Praise for *The Strategy Book*

'A most innovative book. It genuinely synthesises a broad range of strategic thought into a coherent and actionable process. Mckeown brings together a number of apparently incompatible views to create a rich and powerful three dimensional understanding.'
Marcus Alexander, Professor, London Business School

'This is one of the rare strategy books to match lofty ideals with practical action. It gets right down to the business of doing strategy, helping you understand why your strategy works, or not, and what you can do about it. It contains even more nuggets of wisdom than the first edition. And it is very enjoyable to read!'
Manuel Hensmans, Professor of Strategic Management, Toulouse Business School

'Loved the book. So simple, yet so effective. If your bookshelf has a copy of the 1st Edition, dust it off and replace it with the 2nd Edition. Once again the author has pulled off the trick of making something that is thought to be complex and difficult easy to understand and, most of all, apply in the real world. The book retains all the good stuff from the 1st edition, especially its dual nature as a quick read and as a reference book you can return to again and again, and successfully brings it up to date and expands on explanations and examples throughout.'
David Bewick, Nissan Motor Company

'What makes *The Strategy Book* stand out is that it is immediately actionable. Before I could even finish it, we had already begun implementing these ideas in our organisation. Keep this book

close to your desk because you will find yourself returning to its pages again and again.'
Skip Prichard, CEO, OCLC, Leadership Blogger, skipprichard.com

'In this second edition of *The Strategy Book*, Max McKeown achieves yet another masterstroke: he makes complex ideas so readily accessible, practical and engaging that readers will want to apply them. Packed with useful tools and real world examples, this book will be an invaluable aid to anyone looking to develop agile strategic thinking and action in their own organisation.'
Linda Holbeche PhD, Adjunct Professor, Imperial College, London

'Most books on strategy are filled with theory but have few practical steps to help organisations move forward. *The Strategy Book*, on the other hand, is one of my favourite go-to resources to put strategy into action.'
Tony Morgan, Founder and Chief Strategic Officer, The Unstuck Group

'A powerfully practical book for modern strategy analysis. Strongly recommended for people who are interested in developing a profound understanding of their competitive environment.'
Juan Pablo Torres, Professor of Strategy, FEN University of Chile

'Honestly, this has been the best business book I have read. Perhaps best described as a mini MBA! I love how each strategic concept is linked to real case studies which provide great insights about the journey other strategists have been through.'
Eric Lowenstein, Entrepeneur-in-Residence, Aon Plc

'This is my go-to strategy book for teaching and consulting. It's like my favourite carry-on bag: adaptable, thorough and perfectly arranged.'
Dr. Julia Sloan, author of *Learning to Think Strategically*, Columbia University

'This new edition is even clearer than the first one. Max really gets to the heart of why strategic thinking is the bloodline of any business. This book is for those that "do" strategy and are responsible for delivering it. It will help make your strategy a reality.'
Kiran Nobeen, Director of Account Management, EMEA, Ventiv Technology Group

'Max de-clutters corporate speak and opens up strategy to everyone. His no-nonsense approach to corporate strategy will teach you to look at your business like never before. In person, his insight is scalpel sharp, and this book is a masterclass in improving your strategic thinking.'
Steve Fortune, Global Leadership Development, Pfizer

'If you want to become a better strategic thinker, read Max's new book. Succinct and to the point, he captures the essence of strategy. With a passion and style all of his own, he connects insights from leading strategy gurus to successful practices in leading companies.'
Simon Collinson, Professor and Dean, Birmingham Business School

'Max has his own style of talking strategy, crossing all corporate and conventional boundaries. This book is a contribution to strategy for the 21st century. A great book that's fun to read.'
Jan-Henrick Andersson, Vice President, Metro AG

'*The Strategy Book* starts with you – and ends with a plan that shapes your future. It is filled with useful checklists to help you avoid the usual pitfalls and get you on your way. A great read to help you win over and over again.'
Scott Smith, Director, Microsoft, Middle-East

'Max encourages you to engage with strategy and see the world with different eyes. He takes the mystery out of strategic planning. He invites you to adopt an effective, inclusive and collaborative approach, and appreciate that good strategy needs to be flexible

and prepared for unplanned opportunities. If you want to shape your professional future, and you're prepared to ask yourself some challenging questions, I can only recommend this book!'
Jost Wahlen, Head of Learning and Development, Allianz Insurance

'This book is both challenging and fun. Max cuts confidently through the hype and provides a critical and well-rounded view of the challenge of strategic thinking in contemporary business. This book entertains its readers while showing respect to their intelligence.'
Saku Mantere, Professor of Strategy and Organisation, McGill University

'Cuts the cr*p and demystifies strategy – what else do you want? Managers have a reputation for not reading books, and if they do, for not using what they learn. This book makes it hard to do that. It is well laid out; it builds up the ideas simply, but with strong intellectual underpinnings, good stories and practical implementation ideas.'
Stuart C. Palmer, CEO, Five Talents

'Strategy is a word bandied about by many but understood by few. Reading this book will help you become one of the few.'
Stephen Cummings, Professor of Strategy, Victoria University

'Who knew a sometimes abstract, confusing concept could be made so clearly practical? This book challenges with sophisticated simplicity, providing valuable tools and an impressive plethora of examples to hit the ground running. It's so engaging – it opened my eyes.'
Kathleen Ndongmo, Founder, Natural Ever After, Nigeria

'This is a compelling and fascinating read with a clear, structured discussion of many strategy tools and frameworks. Max has written a valuable book for anyone who has to make a strategic decision.'
Catalina Stefanescu, Dean of Faculty, ESMT European School of Management

'This book explains a range of perspectives and tools with admirable clarity. Max encourages readers to ask uncomfortable questions, and then stimulates the inspiration and imagination to answer them effectively. This is a book that disturbs and demystifies in a creatively helpful way.'
Professor David A. Buchanan, Cranfield University

'With an array of fine examples from a wide range of organisations, this book will appeal to practitioners and students alike. It provides a richness and a challenge to the often stultified frameworks which have come to characterise strategy.'
Professor David Wilson, University of Warwick

'Max stresses that strategy is about shaping the future of organisations . . . Shaping the future means setting in motion a flow of events that, as Max says, "depends on context", and "responding to external waves" and "examining turning points in the future".'
David Boje, Professor, New Mexico State University

'My God, a strategy book that actually makes sense. Imagine that . . . In Mckeown's take on strategy, no-nonsense pragmatism meets imagination and adaptive flexibility. It just might be the cheapest form of strategic insurance ever invented.'
Professor Alf Rehn, Abo Akademi University

'*The Strategy Book* totally demystifies strategy for us non-MBA types struggling to keep pace with the growing demands on our creativity and ability to lead from the front. We will refer to it as a working guide to the strategic and planning process.'
Rahim Dawood, Solutions Architect, Long View Systems

'For ages the corporate strategy process has been kept obscure and unreachable for those without a seat in the boardroom. Mckeown offers a view that is succinct and revealing. Soon you will be thinking and acting strategically in your day-to-day activities.'
Cesar Malacon, Founder Member, Strategic Management Forum

'This is a great and truly helpful book which I fully expect to refer back to for years to come. Max has the ability to articulate clearly

the challenges most organisations face and, with consummate swagger, guide you through strategic thinking relevant to you and the job you do.'
Geir Holmer, ex-Director, Business Intelligence Operations, Virgin Media

'*The Strategy Book* gives a clear and concise introduction to some of the main challenges that organisations face. It's a very useful introduction to the subject and a good way to provoke discussion for more experienced managers.'
Mark Thomas, Associate Dean, Grenoble Ecole de Management

'This book reverse-engineers complexity so readers can truly navigate their business, people and lives with clarity and confidence.'
Jennifer Sertl, President, Agility3R

'This book is highly recommended reading and a useful tool. It has a very good structure making it easy to embrace the powerful ideas inside.'
Harri Ohra-aho, Brigadier General, the Finnish Defence Forces

'*The Strategy Book* is like an ocean full of ideas, very easy to apply to my daily strategic work. As an entrepreneur, I am faced with many of the questions Max asks the reader. They are challenging, but absolutely necessary. An excellent, practical toolkit for anyone who wants to be known as a strategic thinker.'
Riita Raesmaa, Senior Advisor and Partner, Accelerando

'Max has crafted a highly practical resource to guide strategy creation and execution in uncertain times. It is easy to read with clear examples from a wide range of industries.'
Conor Neill, Professor, IESE Universidad de Navarra

'Does exactly what it says on the tin – and does it brilliantly. This book will become a well-thumbed favourite.'
Emma Leech, Director of Marketing, Loughborough University

'You can pick it up, read a section, apply what you have learned and then go back to read some more.'
Sue Toon, Chartered Management Institute

'Recommended. Contains a vast array of strategic experience which is pertinent at any level.'
Laura Dziaszyk, Director, Corporate Signpost

'A comprehensive book that simplifies the topic in a way that is accessible and practical. You'll find it easy to read and fun to implement in your own business. You'll want to go through the process together and see what new strategies you take on for next year.'
Ivana Taylor, Small Business Trends

'If you are short of time, and need a practical guide to what strategy is and how it might help you, then this is the book for you. In a little over 200 pages, it's impressive what is covered, and how useful and understandable it all is. If you only read the checklists from each chapter, the book would be worth it.'
Tom Otley, *Business Traveller Review*

'Mckeown has taken every aspect of strategy, maintained the seriousness of the subject, deconstructed its complexities, and rebuilt his findings in a practical, no-nonsense way that makes his book unstuffy and easy-to-read. It's that rare thing: an academic book that informs and entertains in a universally appealing way.'
Joe Cushnan, Retail Confidential

'Small is indeed beautiful when applied to this book. What I found really refreshing was that it starts with you: what you need to do, today, to flex your strategic thinking muscle, and be seen by others as a strategist, whatever your job title or functional area.'
Amanda Holmes, Senior Lecturer, University of Malta

'If a strategy book is any good it should spark ideas as you read. You should be inspired as you go and close the book after each chapter with a few more ideas and renewed enthusiasm. This book absolutely works on this level. Highly recommended.'
James Ball, Oracle Technical Architect

'I've spent too long in the past wading through worthy, scholarly tomes. And that's why I like *The Strategy Book* so much. If you're studying strategy as an academic subject, then certainly read this

book; but if you're involved in developing the strategy of your own organisation, it is a mission critical read.'
Roger Fielding, Birn and Partners, Denmark

'An excellent book with a new style of talking about strategy. Max guides the strategist in a very straightforward way through every step of the strategy process, with examples and lessons from the real world. As I was reading, I felt my own experiences written in this book.'
Joseph Soueidi, Chief Operations Officer, ATEME

'*The Strategy Book* is a must-read for anybody interested in systematically exploring strategy in their organisation. It is very readable, jargon-free, and of enormous practical value for planning and implementing strategy.'
Professor Cary Cooper, Professor, Organisational Psychology, Manchester Business School

The Strategy Book

The Strategy Book

2nd edition

Max Mckeown

Harlow, England • London • New York • Boston • San Francisco • Toronto • Sydney
Auckland • Singapore • Hong Kong • Tokyo • Seoul • Taipei • New Delhi
Cape Town • São Paulo • Mexico City • Madrid • Amsterdam • Munich • Paris • Milan

PEARSON EDUCATION LIMITED
Edinburgh Gate
Harlow CM20 2JE
United Kingdom
Tel: +44 (0)1279 623623
Web: www.pearson.com/uk

First edition published 2012 (print and electronic)
Second edition published in 2016 (print and electronic)
© Maverick & Strong Limited 2012, 2016 (print and electronic)

ISBN: 978–1–292–08440–4 (print)
      978–1–292–08443–5 (PDF)
      978–1–292–08442–8 (eText)
      978–1–292–08441–1 (ePub)

British Library Cataloguing-in-Publication Data
A catalogue record for the print edition is available from the British Library

Library of Congress Cataloging-in-Publication Data
Mckeown, Max, author.
  The strategy book / Max Mckeown. — 2nd edition.
   pages cm
  Includes index.
  ISBN 978-1-292-08440-4 (pbk.)
  1. Strategic planning. I. Title.
  HD30.28.M3842 2015
  658.4'012—dc23

                        2015030495

10 9 8 7 6 5 4 3 2
19 18 17

Print edition typeset in 9pt Stone Serif ITC Pro by Lumina Datamatics
Printed by Ashford Colour Press Ltd, Gosport

NOTE THAT ANY PAGE CROSS REFERENCES REFER TO THE PRINT EDITION

Contents

About the author

Dr Max Mckeown works as a strategy and innovation coach for many of the most admired and ambitious companies in the world.

The Strategy Book was the winner of the Commuter Read at the Chartered Management Institute Book of the Year 2013 and Amazon's Best Business Books of 2012. Max is also author of the award-winning *The Innovation Book* as well as *Adaptability: The Art of Winning in an Age of Uncertainty*, and four other books. He is also a popular keynote speaker at conferences and events worldwide.

Max has an MBA and PhD from Warwick Business School. He can be reached at www.maxmckeown.com and on twitter@ maxmckeown

First words

'*However beautiful the strategy, you should occasionally look at the results.*'

Winston Churchill

Strategy is about moving from where you are to where you want to be. Smart strategy is the shortest route to desirable ends with available means. Strategy is as much about deciding what to do, where to go, why, when and how as about choosing what not to do. Yes. No. What if. Why not. Planning backwards from a better future.

This book is about strategy in action. It's about making strategic principles and cutting-edge research useful. The second edition includes even more real world examples of strategy in action. You will also find more on new ideas in strategy. Sustainability. Tensions. Psychology. Behavioural strategy. And how to combine creativity and entrepreneurship.

Our human world is the result of individual strategies. Our desires and actions, dreams and ideas. Strategists are able to see the past, present and future as connected. You can link your actions with the actions of those around you. And you will be able to shape events by reacting intelligently and spontaneously to them.

'*All men can see these tactics whereby I conquer, but what none can see is the strategy out of which victory is evolved.*'

Sun Tzu

Max Mckeown

Introduction

What can *The Strategy Book* do for you? This book can help you understand strategy. You can use the secrets in this book to become an effective strategic thinker and leader. If you are ambitious, you can use the powerful strategy tools in this book to *shape your future*.

The Strategy Book has its own strategic advantage. It is easy to read without dumbing down its strategic ideas. It is simple to use but is still based on a core set of intelligent strategic foundations. It offers clear explanations of tools that will help make sense of complex leadership situations.

The Strategy Book is based on hard-won experience and knowledge. I've worked with some of the most admired companies in the world. I've also worked with smaller companies who are some of the most ambitious companies in the world. Some were feeling complacent. Others were facing problems and crisis points. All of them wanted more success.

The Strategy Book helps with all of those situations. And it also helps people who are studying strategy as part of a course or degree. A lot of the books you have to study are either too shallow or far too long. This book is about giving you the best ideas in strategy but wrapped up in a usable, enjoyable package.

How to use this book

The Strategy Book is organised into six parts. The first five parts tackle the really important challenges that a leader of any team of any size will face in creating strategy and making that strategy work. Each part is sub-divided into specific action topics. You can dip in and out of each section as you feel relevant. They have been written clearly so that you can benefit from my experience as a strategist whether you are a novice or an expert.

Each of the action topics has the following structure:

- *Headline description* – so you know what the topic is about, why it's important and have a brief summary of how the contents will help.

- *Strategic examples* – so you can read about a successful company or person that faced the same kind of challenge and used the same kind of principles to solve their problems. This is a powerful and memorable way to learn.

- *Strategy ratings* – so you have an idea how important the principle is in your work as a strategic thinker. The Strategy6 are six particularly valuable principles, and can be found on pages 4, 27, 56, 120 and 127. This section also lets you know how often a strategic challenge will be used and who should be involved.

- *Objective* – why you should take the subject seriously as a leader and what you should be trying to achieve.

- *Context* – how the subject fits into the broader pattern of leadership and the kind of situation you are dealing with to achieve success.

- *Challenge* – why the subject is difficult and valuable. And also ways of succeeding with the challenge effectively as a strategist.

- *Success* – what has to happen to succeed with the challenge.

- *Strategists' measure of success* – ways you can assess your progress.

- *Strategists' checklist* – a summary of the actions you have to take to put the strategy principle into action.

- *Related ideas* – some suggestions of other writers' ideas that support or complement the strategic topic.

The sixth part is the strategist's toolkit. The most important models and tools of strategy are explained in very precise, practical and efficient terms. You can move from the toolkit to the action topics.

Or you can move from specific action topics back to models that help you to organise your thoughts.

There is also a list of further reading if you want to dig deeper. And naturally there is an index to make it easier to find your way to specific topics.

The Strategy Book is clearly structured and easy to use, something that you will find yourself referring back to again and again.

What is strategy?

Strategy is about shaping the future – it is about how people attain desirable ends with available means. That's the reason we're interested. And that's the best definition I can offer you. But as a strategist it can also help to understand some of the different arguments about what strategy is and isn't. You don't have to know the whole history. You don't have to get a doctorate or an MBA. But it's helpful to be informed.

Frequency: Read first, review occasionally.
Key participants: First, you. Then, everyone.
Strategy rating: Strategy6

Google made the decision to give their engineers permission to experiment in free time. They used this free time to produce an online video service. This experiment taught executives the importance of online video so they bought YouTube as a priority when it became popular. As a result, they still have two of the most popular search services in the world. Not really a plan, yet all about opportunity. Was this creative strategy at work?

Objective

There are some benefits to understanding the history of strategy as it's usually told in business schools and text books. It helps you to discuss strategy knowledgeably and to see its limitations – as well as its purpose.

Ancient strategy. The word strategy has its origins in the Greek word *strategos*, which means general or someone who has an army (*stratos*) to lead. It was first used in Athens (508 BC) to describe the art of leadership used by the ten generals on the war council. They developed principles of effective leadership and achieving objectives. This included approaches to war and motivating soldiers.

Similar concepts about strategy emerged in Asia, most famously in Sun Tzu's *Art of War* (written 200 BC), which is still bought by people today. In his book, Sun Tzu lists different principles that leaders may follow to win and achieve their goals. It set a pattern for books about strategy that is still followed. Experienced executives and consultants share their experience of planning for success.

Corporate strategy started getting a lot of attention from the 1950s. It was only after the Second World War that strategy books appeared for business leaders.

Alfred Chandler was a historian who, in the 1960s, examined the relationship between strategy and organisational structure. He concluded that the strategy chosen by the company will lead to changes in the structure of the company. His work also shows that strategy was not a new concept in business since it was based on what companies were already doing.

Igor Ansoff was a manager and mathematician often described as the father of strategic management. His book, *Corporate Strategy*, was published in 1965 and was a comprehensive attempt to explain how managers could plan for a more successful future.

Ansoff was the most prominent writer of an approach to strategy that became obsessed with detailed planning. It was a perfect fit to a management style that was all about control. It led to a view that CEOs could work with strategic planning teams to analyse the past to predict the future. Early computers were used to help crunch the numbers and print the plans used to issue orders to real people in middle management and the front lines.

Henry Mintzberg is a Canadian professor and contrarian who mocked planning obsession. He argued that only some strategic plans ever happened the way they were intended. The big picture – or strategy – was decided by a stream of individual actions. He believed that most strategy emerges from adaptation. Arguments between planning and learning approaches continue today (see page 213).

Michael Porter (also a professor) continued the mathematical approach to strategy. For him, strategy was about detailed analysis with clear models. These models were designed to determine what position the company should take in relation to other competitors in the market (see pages 169–73).

Context

In some ways, the intellectual history of strategy is more complex than my short introduction. Yet in other ways, it's simpler. Some argue for the more creative, human side, while others argue for the more analytical side of strategy. Both are important, so a strategist asks what balance of these approaches is most helpful in any particular situation.

- What are you doing at the moment?
- How does that compare to your competitors?
- What do you want to achieve?
- How can you create something people want?

The first two questions are analytical, they are about positioning and benchmarking. The second set of questions are creative, and are about desire and contribution. They are interrelated but the balance between them varies. The balance depends on your personal preferences and circumstances.

Challenge

If your market is stable and you're happy with your situation then you may choose to keep planning and adapting in a predictable way. But if your market is dynamic and you want your situation to change, then you may choose to inject more creativity into improving what you offer and achieve.

This book includes tools for both analytical and creative strategy. It also includes my opinion that creative, dynamic strategy is the more helpful approach to take. The analytical tools can be used creatively to contribute something worthwhile and – if you wish – difficult to copy.

Success

You'll know that you understand the principle when you see the difference between creative and analytical approaches to strategy. You will also be able to combine the tools (see page 163) and the principles throughout this book to think like a strategist about the bigger picture and what you want to contribute.

You can study everything from ideas about how to run a strategy meeting to why reacting is more important than planning, to specific strategies that you can choose to use or adapt. The overall aim is to improve your ability to do something worthwhile. Something better than merely sustaining competitive edge.

Strategists' measures of success

- The basic origins of modern corporate strategy are understood.
- The difference between creative and analytical strategy is recognised.
- Creative and analytical tools and principles are used together.
- Stable and dynamic markets are treated differently.
- You know there is more to strategy than beating or copying your competitors.

Pitfalls

Over reliance on any particular approach to strategy is dangerous. You are missing the big picture if you believe that you can ignore analysis, creativity or the action that makes creativity and analysis come to life. Your organisation may have a traditional approach to strategy. You will have to look carefully at how well the approach is working and what improvements can be made.

Strategists' checklist

- Consider the differences between analytical and creative strategy.

- Think about whether your company takes a more analytical or more creative approach.

- Explore whether the traditional approach is well suited to the environment you are facing.

- Keep referring back to the basic distinction as you proceed through the book so you don't forget that all tools can be used in both ways.

- Introduce both analytical and creative approaches to your team. Discuss how they have been used in the past and how you could alter the balance in the future.

Related ideas

Richard Whittington argues that 'strategy is hard'. If strategy was easy, every company would succeed, but they don't. The important part is to learn how to think better and think differently. He introduces four schools of strategy: '*Classical*', which seeks to maximise profit with deliberate processes; '*Evolutionary*', which seeks to maximise profit with emergent processes; '*Systematic*', which seeks plural objectives with deliberate processes; and '*Processual*', which has plural objectives with emergent processes.

Regardless of which approach you take, John McGee, professor at Warwick Business School, argues that strategic decisions often have certain characteristics. Such decisions will involve risk because you are betting on a future that is uncertain and complex with preparations that are also uncertain and complex. Some strategic preparations require considerable time, effort, and even pain, before any long-term benefit comes your way. Yet smart strategists, as the next chapter will explain, know that because events may prove you wrong, reacting may be as important as planning.

one

Your strategic self

Strategy is about shaping the future. But it doesn't always work in the real world. And that's the reason for this book – to help you to use strategy to figure out what to do now to get what you really want later. This book can help make strategy work more often.

There are strategy tools and processes that can help, but the real heart of strategy is the strategist. It's what you know, how you think, and how you get people to care enough about what you are doing to achieve your goals.

It's also about setting in motion the sequence of events that will shape the future in a way that you like. The more you understand the people who make events happen and the connections between what they do and those events, the smarter you will be.

You have already used strategy to get a lot of what you have. You got a job. Or you got an education to get a job. You might have saved money for a holiday or a home. Maybe you romanced your partner, wife or husband.

You did something in the past to try to get something better in the future.

Becoming a strategic thinker – a strategist – is about getting better at shaping events. In the business world you need to understand how strategy is usually done. You need to know how to create strategy that convinces others to support you (including your boss or shareholders). And you need to know how to make strategy deliver success in the real world. Strategy that works.

There is no guarantee that the future will turn out the way you want. Just writing a plan does not mean that the plan will happen. The world is more complex than our ability to plan, but that's part of what an effective strategist learns to accept. You learn that reacting and responding to events is just as important as planning.

Some business schools and consultancies have sold the promise that strategy can solve everything. In their hands, strategy has become a cult that believes in the magical power of a few models. They have taken away from the art of strategy and left some non-MBAs wondering if there is any room for entrepreneurial instinct.

Others have become cynical about strategy. They hear the word and disengage. They expect bad or boring things to come from any strategic planning process. They predict job cuts or mindless changes. Or just expect meaningless waffle that means nothing in the real world. And there is some truth to this view.

Yet we have been trying to shape our future for as long as we have been human. It is in our nature to interpret our experience to provide shortcuts for a better future. This is what strategy is about and how it can be of value in the real world.

To become an effective strategist, you need to start with yourself. Begin by understanding how one thing leads to another. Get yourself an education in the basics of strategy tools and models. Pay more attention to where you are, what's happening around you, and how trends create opportunities to get to where you want to be.

Shaping the future

Strategy is about shaping the future. Corporate strategy is about shaping the future for an organisation. You use strategy to figure out how to achieve your purpose and ambitions. You move between where you want to go (ends) and what you need to do to get there (means). Great strategy is the quickest route from available means to desirable ends to shape your future.

Frequency: Every problem, every opportunity!
Key participants: The whole organisation.
Strategy rating: Strategy6

The Cheesecake Factory has grown into a billion dollar corporation. Its recipe for success is based on a small number of strategic ingredients. The founder created a 'unique concept with the broadest, deepest menu in casual dining' and the best cheesecake he could make. They spend $2000 per employee just on training to make sure people deliver the best customer experience.

They open new restaurants when they find wonderful new locations, rather than just because they have money to spend or bonuses to earn. They focus improvement efforts on increasing taste, with quality homemade cooking and fast preparation, rather than reducing cost. This patience and discipline is about doing what makes long-term sense.

These are strategic decisions. They are not accidental, although they did not all come from planning. They are part of a strategic package. They shape the competitive environment. They stop copycats. And they shape the future in ways that are desirable and believable to customers, investors, managers and employees.

Objective

Shaping the future of an organisation involves every part and everyone. Strategy considers things inside and outside the organisation that will make a difference to its success. The strategist also looks for opportunities and threats to the future of the organisation. Ideally these are explored with imagination, ambition and a creative understanding of customers, products and resources.

To shape the future requires a combination of thinking, planning and reacting to events that emerge along the way. These provide key strategy questions:

- What do we want to do?
- What do we think is possible?
- What do we need to do to achieve our goals?
- When should we react to new opportunities and adapt plans?

What do we want to do?

This establishes a sense of what is desirable. Organisations tend to have an overall purpose. Sometimes the purpose is very precise and deliberately agreed. Sometimes the purpose of the organisation is very ambiguous. There may be many different opinions about what the organisation is for and what it should do. These opinions may conflict and compete with each other. This is all of interest to the strategic thinker.

What do we think is possible?

This introduces some sense of practicality. You look at opportunities in the world contrasted with the resources that the organisation either has or can obtain. But looking at opportunities can also expand a sense of what is possible beyond what has been done in the past. What do the achievements of others and trends in technology and consumer desires allow your company to do next?

What do we need to do to achieve our goals?

This includes the necessary strategic moves to achieve the overall goals of the organisation. It includes the style of leadership, the structures and processes of the organisation. And the projects, tasks, roles, products and services that have to be done to achieve organisational aspirations. Ideally these actions work together in some – more or less – harmonious way so that the sum of actions is greater than their parts.

When should we react to new opportunities and adapt plans?

Our views of the future are incomplete. When we write our plans or decide on an overall purpose we don't really know what is going to happen next. Small and big events will happen that challenge the existing strategy. New opportunities will emerge that are bigger, better or just different from those we thought of the first time.

Context

Shaping the future depends on context. You can't control the waves of human desire and endeavour with strategy, but you can create strategy that surfs those human waves, contributing to them or benefiting from them. It follows that you need to understand the context for any attempt to create strategy.

There are probably some low competition, high stability places in the world. But it is safer to assume that the external context your strategy will face will be high competition, low stability. So this book will make the same assumption and give advice on strategy that can be effective in such a world.

Each section answers questions that are needed to create a strategy that can be used to shape the future. There are sections that explain how to create strategy, think like a strategist, win with strategy, make your strategy work, build a strategic organisation and troubleshoot your strategy whenever it stops working.

Challenge

A lot of organisations still set in motion grand plans to a better future. The larger the organisation, even now, the more likely it is that they have a strategic planning team who produce strategy documents as a result of lengthy financial analysis.

This plan is then 'cascaded' or passed down the hierarchy until it reaches middle management, at which point it often disappears. The front line may have to work in structures, processes or role descriptions that were designed as part of the plan. This planning, command and control approach often leads to out-of-date strategy and out-of-touch leaders.

Some people argue it isn't even possible to plan because events are so unpredictable. They claim it is better to just organise as efficiently as possible. Then you just hope evolutionary market forces (what people want interacting with what people sell) will be a natural fit to whatever you are doing.

The trouble with this evolutionary approach is that it doesn't really address what you need to *try* to do to make it more likely that your company is a natural fit. And that's why clever strategy is somewhere between the extremes. It does try to plan deliberate actions to shape the future, but also tries to stay close to local events and to react to them. In this way, strategy is transformed into a learning process that becomes – at its best – smarter through experimentation.

Success

Progress is made when the organisation moves towards strategy that learns its lessons and adapts to new opportunities. In this way, you can benefit from strategic thinking that is clever rather than one-size-fits-all strategy. You will also see people at all levels more involved because managers are interested in what is really happening at the front line.

Your strategy efforts will use strategic principles and tools to better prepare the organisation for shaping the future. Your strategy will craft a response to external waves, needs of customers and actions of competitors. Your strategy will consider the nature of the business (its purpose, style and products) and the ways that it organises internal resources, processes and people.

Strategists' measures of success

→ Understand (and apply) the main strategy questions.

→ Use the differences between planning, coping, adapting and shaping covered throughout this book.

> Consider a wide range of internal and external aspects.

> Accept the need to build a strategic organisation to achieve shared purpose.

> Establish a flexible, continuous approach to strategy.

Pitfalls

It's important that efforts to introduce more strategy don't lead to less strategic thinking (or worse results). There are lots of naturally strategic people who see opportunities, see new patterns and adjust the work of the organisation to take advantage of these. It's also important not to simply replace one set of words with another. The idea of strategic thinking is to improve results.

Strategists' checklist

▓ Remember that inward-looking planning is not sufficient because of the high levels of external change and competition.

▓ Work your way through the strategy questions (see page 165) and answer them for your business. This provides a valuable template for developing creative strategy that is straightforward enough for all sizes of business.

▓ Understand the importance of a learning approach to strategy. This means that as many people as possible are engaged with strategy so that they can adapt what they do to support the purpose of the organisation. And so that they can feed back valuable information to their leadership team in order to adapt the official strategy.

Related ideas

For Professors Howard Thomas and Taïeb Hafsi, strategy is a mixture of rules of thumb and creative methods. It helps people understand and transform reality. This means that strategy tools are only valuable if they stay close to reality. Some techniques are useful only for making specific decisions. The most powerful tools will help people navigate the process of shaping the future. Without this, strategy is nothing. It's worth remembering that the actions of people in organisations can be the result of habits, hypothesis or heuristics. Any of these actions can have strategic consequences. This is particularly true for deep patterns of actions that shape what – and how – an organisation behaves.

As an example, research by Bingham and Eisenhardt, professors at North Carolina and Stanford, introduces the idea that organisations develop a 'portfolio of heuristics'. These are lessons, helpful and unhelpful, that come from experience that shape actions. Some of these lessons become an embedded and unquestioned part of culture. Hypothesis can help challenge both habits and heuristics where necessary.

For similar reasons, Richard Rumelt argues, in his best-selling book *Good Strategy, Bad Strategy*, that the key thing is to have a diagnosis and guiding policy connected to a set of coherent (real world) actions. He concludes that bad strategy is fluff, while good strategy is logic – although you should note that smart strategy is often ultimately a form of fuzzy logic that must adapt to messy, real world situations.

Thinking *before* you plan

Strategy is about out-thinking your competition. It's about vision first and planning second. That's why it's so important that you think *before* you plan. And that the thinking part of what you do is given priority. Strategists who don't take time to think are just planners.

Frequency: Before, during and after planning.
Key participants: Everyone needs to think, but this starts with you.
Strategy rating: ***

Mark Zuckerberg, while at Harvard, built a website called Facemash 'for fun'. He built it over the weekend. He built it without permission. It allowed visitors to choose who was 'hotter' from photos of two people. It was a copy of an already existing idea and it was shut down. So he decided to build something *better* and launched Facebook from his dorm room. Thinking came first – what fun stuff *could* be done and why – then the planning. Even today, Facebook believes that 'done is better than perfect'. And that's how creative strategic thinking works best.

Done strategically is often better than operationally perfect. Zuckerberg continues to educate analysts about the long-term thinking that guides Facebook's actions. In this way, he gains long-term supporters who have done their own thinking before investment. Buying Instagram for $1 billion, over one Easter weekend, or WhatsApp for $21 billion, were completed not because it was planned but *because* Facebook had already done so much strategic thinking. They knew how the investments could help them prepare for the future. It's a think first, plan later approach.

Objective

Planning takes time. It's serious work and it's relatively unimaginative (and uninspiring). It has to be that way because planning is about getting things done. It's a practical part of organising effort.

Tasks are listed, project teams formed, and complex project charts and checklists are created.

But if you start the planning *before* thinking, you can end up with the wrong solution to the right problem. Or perhaps the right solution to the wrong problem. Or the least imaginative solution to a really important problem.

You might miss out on all the creative ways you could have grabbed the very biggest opportunities. Your objective should be to make sure that imaginative, open, playful, passionate thinking happens *before* the serious work of planning begins. That's what strategy is about – *thinking* strategically.

Your objective should be to stay as open as possible before you get down to the realistic business of planning. You'll find that it's just as easy to plan something amazing as it is to plan something obvious.

Context

Strategy is about the shortest route between means and ends. It's either about out-thinking the competition or, even better, about finding new, even greater opportunities. Opportunities the competition hasn't found yet. Or opportunities the competition doesn't understand because it hasn't done the kind of thinking that you have.

There are always better ways of doing anything. There are always shorter routes for getting from where you are to where you want to be. There are always new markets that are growing faster than your market. There are forever methods, relationships and ideas just waiting to be discovered, and these can only be discovered by creating room – slack – for thinking.

Throughout *The Strategy Book* there are questions you should be thinking about. They are thought experiments to be done alone and also in groups. You don't need to try out every plan in practice; you need to test a range of plans in your mind. You need to explore what is possible so you can extend what is possible. That is the essential value of strategic thinking against just working hard. It requires you to question what is being done and what could be done.

Challenge

There are lots of reasons why organisations don't think before they plan. The most important given is probably the lack of time. People say they are so busy planning, organising, doing and coping with problems that they don't have time for thinking. Thinking is a luxury they wish they had time for, but don't.

Some people feel thinking is an *unnecessary* luxury. For action-oriented individuals, it may seem obvious what they should be doing. The more pressing questions are how efficiently they can organise the work and how effectively they can get people to do the work.

Experience with ineffective bureaucracy can also reduce people's patience with attempts at spending time thinking. Painful brainstorming, meetings from hell and hierarchies replete with steering committees make everything to do with strategy unattractive to those who want to get things done.

Successful organisations try to have a healthy balance between thinking, planning and doing. They spend time learning from what they have done before and how well their plans have led to the results that they intended. They also just explore their world without specific plans in mind. It's worth asking a few questions:

- How much time have you invested in thinking about strategy?
- How many options have you considered before the plan was written?
- How have you ensured that the thinking behind the plan is challenged?
- How much time do you spend exploring trends, possibilities and cool stuff? How much time is spent playing with ideas, hopes and dreams?

Success

You'll know that you're getting better at thinking before planning when there is time for thinking built into your corporate calendar and, just as importantly, into your personal timetable. It doesn't need to be excessive – the idea is to find an effective balance, but that means more than a couple of days a year.

Thinking about strategy is not just for the people who like to think about strategy. So success will also be measured by the range of people you involve in the thinking and questioning that comes before strategy.

- Is the whole team taking an active part in thinking sessions?
- Are the different departments and functions included?
- Is the complete organisation included in the thinking process?
- Are people outside the organisation (and customers) included?

Asking demanding questions about the plans, results and thinking of the past will become an acceptable (even necessary) part of how the organisation works. More importantly, time spent creatively exploring possibilities and opportunities will be viewed as valuable activity. Challenging prevailing wisdom will be given the room it deserves and those who ask difficult questions will be protected.

Strategists' measures of success

- You understand the thinking that got your company to where it is now.
- Thinking is built into your strategy and planning process.
- Different thought experiments happen before planning and action.
- You recognise the value of thinking as a distinct part of strategic success.
- Your company knows how to challenge its own thinking and actions.
- You stay with problems (and opportunities) long enough to make progress.

Pitfalls

Telling people to think *before* they plan can lead to problems. Some may conclude that you're trying to slow down meaningful action. One risk is that urgency is reduced by those who don't want to move to action. Another is that those who want action fight against the thinking because they believe it's wasted time. It's important to clarify the benefits of thinking *before* planning and to build it into specific stages of the strategy through to the action process.

........' checklist

- Remember that the best strategy is about thinking your way to new possibilities from where you are currently. Planning comes next.

- Improving strategy means improving your ability to think, not just your intelligence, or your knowledge, but the ways in which you think.

- Establish time for thinking in your schedule. And include time for thinking in the normal schedule for your team, department or organisation. Particularly before the start of new planning efforts.

- Avoid having just one plan (or set of options) to follow. Try several different courses of action. Experiment with them using imagination to see what advantages each route forward offers.

- Bring in external people to challenge (and examine) your thinking. It's important that they don't just agree with whatever you have planned. The thinking and assumptions that went into your plans are then tested again before the months of action that follow.

Related ideas

Chris Argyris' ideas are useful here. Strategic planning is like single-loop learning. You do something, wait until it's finished, and then figure out what worked and what didn't. Strategic thinking is like double-loop learning. You think through what might happen, and what is happening, and use imagination to learn lessons while there is still time to change (see page 211).

As Sir Lawrence Freedman states, in his book *Strategy: A History*, 'a gifted strategist' will keep moving between ends and means. The smart strategist will cycle between present opportunities and future possibilities. Clever actions made with ends in mind, so each action you take increases the range of desirable outcomes and the likelihood of them happening.

Becoming a strategic thinker

Becoming a strategic thinker is about opening your mind to possibilities. It's about seeing the bigger picture. It's about understanding the various parts of your business, taking them apart, and then putting them back together again in a more powerful way. It's about insight, invention, emotion and imagination focused on reshaping some part of the world.

Frequency: Every problem, every opportunity!
Key participants: You.
Strategy rating: *****

At the age of 11, Taylor Swift realised her talent for singing was not enough when she failed to get a record deal. To succeed, she decided to be strategically different. Learning three guitar chords won her a song-writing deal with Sony aged fifteen. Modelling for Abercrombie & Fitch increased her profile. Instinctive use of social media expanded her fan base. Writing songs from her teenage perspective produced a No. 1 album few other people could have created. She has made a series of ambitious, strategic moves. She collaborated with other musical stars to give her appeal beyond country pop. Strategic thinking has taken her from karaoke competitions to one of the world's most powerful musicians.

Objective

It's possible to be a strategic thinker without using any strategy tools, but it's not possible to create brilliant strategy without being a strategic thinker. There is an important difference between creating strategy documents and creating strategy that gets you where you want to be. There's also a valuable difference between managerial thinking and strategic thinking.

Leaders often say they want strategic thinking. They want to be prepared and they believe strategic thinking will help them prepare. They want more from less, and they depend on strategic thinking to deliver. They want people around them who see the bigger picture. They want clever solutions to messy problems. And they want to move beyond the obvious and out-think the competition.

Strategic thinkers ask different kinds of questions and look at old (and new) problems with fresh eyes. They see what other people miss – whether that's some apparently unimportant detail or some very long-term trend as part of a much bigger picture. Part of their value is that they ask questions that are creative and custom-made for the particular situation. This book is full of questions to give you more options when you are forming your own strategic questions. But the most important questions to keep asking are: why and why not?

- Why not change the rules?
- Why do we do what we're doing?
- Why are we happy (or not) with the status quo?
- Why not do something (completely) different?
- Why will our plan work (or fail)?

It's best to focus on questions that open up thinking rather than prematurely landing in unhelpful levels of operational detail. The strategic thinker is able to open up thinking (creating lots of possibilities) and then create visions that are clear and engaging to shape the future in desirable ways.

Context

Organisations tend to be full of people trapped by a series of constraints. Their view of the world is limited by role descriptions, departmental responsibilities and corporate processes. In addition, their focus tends to be on the short-term demands of reporting structures and performance management.

Different people are naturally interested in different aspects of the big picture. Some focus on practical aspects of what happens next, others want to understand the facts and figures to support a new direction. Some are concerned about its impact on people (the wider team) while others want to do something new and amazing whether or not it is realistic or practical.

The strategic thinker is interested in aspects of all of these concerns but is capable of a kind of mental gymnastics. Strategic thinkers are able to link ideas from different specialist areas and highlight opportunities from contradiction, tension and paradox. They work out how things can fit together better.

Challenge

In times of stability or straightforward growth, bold strategic thinkers can be underappreciated. They want to do great things and when they are stopped they either give up or move on. In times of uncertainty, or when it becomes hard to grow, the organisation urgently needs strategic thinkers but may find that it doesn't have enough of those people in positions of influence. It may also find that it's not used to listening to them (or joining in the strategic conversation) so that they have to learn new strategic thinking habits.

Another challenge is that there is very little formal development of strategic thinking that includes the kind of creative, obsessive eclecticism that is necessary. Part of the reason is that it's just not easy to do. You can't just have dull, uninspired, by-the-numbers, check-box training for strategic thinking if you want to have brilliant, inspired, beyond the numbers, out of the box behaviour.

The good news is that most people *want* to be creative and have a desire to understand how to improve their future. There are many sources of inspiration for strategic thinking – what people hate, what they love, what frustrates them, what captivates them. And strategic thinking can turn disconnected emotions, desire and effort into something that offers direction and purpose.

Success

You'll know when you're getting better at strategic thinking when your first response to a situation is to ask open questions. You will start trying to take things apart that seem closed and then putting them back together. You will become more playful and creative with the combinations that you try. And you will look for more varied, eclectic, diverse inputs into your thinking process.

- How does your industry (or sector) work?
- What does success look like for your organisation?
- What would it take to do ten times better?
- What is the most important (root) issue you face?
- What would you do with no limitations?
- How many of those limitations are real?
- What are older, younger, richer or poorer people doing?

As a leader you will become less interested in conformity because you know that conformity has limited value. You will become impatient with 'me-too', copy-cat plans and strategies. You will ask for the 'next big thing'. And you will invest in people and work that is ambitious and bold. It's often no harder to grow than to shrink as an organisation, and you choose growth.

Strategists' measures of success

- See beyond the obvious to new possibilities for the big picture.
- Understand how to break down a situation into smaller pieces.
- Know how to play with individual parts and reorganise them.
- Be aware of the most important strategy tools and principles.
- Gain the ability to create vision and goals beyond the short-term.
- The people around you acknowledge you as a strategic thinker.

Pitfalls

Regardless of your role, in a corporate environment you're going to need to have a strategy to sell your ability as a strategic thinker. You want people to acknowledge and understand your ability. It's easy to irritate or frustrate others if you proclaim yourself to be a strategic thinker. It's better to develop your skills (and reputation) by applying them first to your work and then to how to share your hard-won knowledge with others.

Strategists' checklist

- Become skilled at using questions to guide your strategic thinking. Use *Why?* and *Why not?* as a starting point, along with the other questions in this book and new, imaginative questions that you create to find opportunity in your particular situation.

- Understand the difference between strategic planning and strategic thinking (see the previous section) so you keep pushing for that powerful combination of practicality and intuition.

- Move from breaking down a problem to building it back up into a better understanding of the problem, and then into a strategic response to the problem that creates new possibilities.

- Become adept at using the various tools and principles in this book. They have been selected to develop strategic thinking and are intended to encourage their use in creative, bold, flexible ways that inspire.

Related ideas

Kenichi Ohmae, in his classic book *The Mind of the Strategist*, argues that managers tend to focus too much on beating (or copying) competitors. The open mind of the strategic thinker can choose to look for ambitious, new ways of creating wealth that focus on the (unmet) needs of customers and the strengths of their own organisations.

In a recent article for *American Psychology*, Daniel Kahneman, author of *Thinking, Fast and Slow*, and Gary Klein, author of *Seeing What Others Don't*, debated the relative benefits and dangers of intuition. They agreed that smart strategic thinkers guard themselves against the pitfalls of bias by recognising the limits of gut decisions. They consider what might go wrong by conducting what Klein describes as 'premortems'. Overconfidence is dangerous, particularly because leaders may gain power because of lucky risk taking, rather than wisdom.

Selling your strategy

Corporate strategy is usually only useful if you get people engaged with helping you to make it work. You have to explain your strategic ideas to the leadership team to get them to support your ideas, and you will have to communicate and involve people at all levels. Selling is often the forgotten part of the strategy process – the part that convinces people that the strategy is a credible and worthwhile way of shaping the future.

Frequency: At the start then regularly.
Key participants: Leadership team, then everyone.
Strategy rating: **

Sony put an outsider in charge of its next generation games console. This happened only after that outsider successfully pointed out previous strategic mistakes and put himself forward for the job of strategist. An American software guy who went to gamers, and developers, to ask what they wanted, and then successfully sold the 'For the Gamers' strategy to the Sony leadership. Selling the strategy was hard work, but the result was a product that was easy to develop for, and fun to play. The PS4 has been a strategic triumph, profitably out-selling its rivals almost two to one.

Unfortunately, the new Microsoft console was much less about the gamers, and much more about the CEO telling, rather than selling, his strategy. They wanted to 'own the living-room'. Every corporate aspiration and objective got thrown into one product. Every executive got a piece of the action, without strategic arguments that made sense outside of the boardroom. The result was a console that was more expensive, and less profitable, than the PS4. They had repeated Sony's previous generation of mistakes, for almost the same reasons.

Objective

To get the company to follow your strategy, you'll have to get the leadership team to endorse it. You don't have to start with the top team. In fact, you don't usually get the opportunity to pitch directly without some effort campaigning for it.

Fortunately, you can develop your strategy while engaging people with it so that momentum builds. Better to treat strategic ideas as part of a conversation if you really want to move the direction of your organisation. The same approach will help if you just want to get involved in shaping its future and be accepted as a strategic thinker. You need to be able to sell strategy.

Not all strategy needs billions in investment, but strategy needs support from a larger group than the person who came up with the idea. At some point you'll probably need the endorsement of senior management, and you're certain to need the support of various people in (and outside) the company if they are to make your strategy work. At some point, strategy must engage action.

Context

First, consider what your strategy needs to work. Then you can work backwards to where you are and figure out how to get what your strategy needs. Go over the logic of your strategy. Use the tools and techniques in this book to construct a strategy that can take advantage of opportunities and deal with probable threats of various kinds.

Second, give serious thought to why your company should care about your strategy. Specifically, find problems that the board want to be solved. What are senior managers scared of? What are they talking about? What problems does your strategy solve? What problems does your strategy solve that your leadership team understands? What kind of strategy are they ready to buy?

If your strategy needs support outside of your control, then you have to take the selling process seriously. Many talented people with powerful ideas that would have helped the organisation don't know how to sell those ideas. So you either need to get better at selling ideas, or find someone else who can sell them with you.

- What is the formal strategy planning process in your organisation?
- How do ideas (and strategic ideas) get funding and support?
- What is the informal decision-making process?
- Who are the strategic influencers in your organisation?
- When is the best time to sell strategic ideas?

The answers to these questions will be different for every organisation. Part of becoming a credible strategic thinker is learning effective approaches to selling ideas for your situation. Usually, a mixture of formal and informal influencing is necessary, as well as a mixture of passion, logic, creativity and financial details to gain the support your strategy needs.

Challenge

The specifics of selling a strategy depend on where you work and how you fit into the pecking order. There is a difference in levels of formality and process in different places. There is also a difference in how you get noticed if you are at the bottom, middle, or top of the organisation.

Some of your choices depend on where you want to focus your strategic thinking. There are many good reasons for starting with strategy that will help your immediate job and your team. It's a good way of developing the skills you need and your working knowledge of the tools that can help you. It's also an effective way of building credibility *before* asking people to invest in bigger ideas that affect the whole company.

There may be exceptions. An enlightened leadership team may believe strategy should include ideas and engagement from everyone. Find out if that's true in principle and test it in practice with smaller suggestions to see what happens. Look around to see if anyone has successfully influenced the direction of the company from outside the senior management levels.

You may decide that your ideas are too urgent to wait. Perhaps you are personally so passionate about your strategic ideas that you are willing to adopt an all-or-nothing approach. You may be so convinced by your ideas that you are willing to leave to put them into practice. You may feel that the situation facing the company is so desperate that it is now or never.

And you may just stumble into an opportunity to pitch strategy that is too good to ignore. Reacting to opportunities is important to real-world strategy so don't let me stop you. Just take a moment to consider your options.

Success

You'll know that you're getting better at selling (or pitching) strategy when managers start coming to you when there is strategic thinking to be done. And you'll really know that you're getting good when you are able to shape strategy in your organisation. Your influencing skills will help in engaging people with the future at all levels, inside and outside of the organisation.

Your strategic ideas will come with options, so that people can choose between them. You will be able to pitch ideas that are clear enough to be understood but flexible enough for people to contribute to them. You will be able to use stories to engage emotions while using numbers to make your strategic ideas concrete and credible.

Strategists' measures of success

→ You know how strategy is created and put into practice in your organisation.

→ You are actively improving your pitching and influencing skills.

→ You have your own opinion on existing and future strategy.

→ Other people invite you to share your opinion and make a contribution.

Pitfalls

No one likes to feel manipulated, so be careful with crass use of influencing techniques. No one likes a know-it-all either, so do more listening as you learn to be part of the strategic conversation. Remember that there are hidden games being played. Some games are just normal human ways of reaching decisions. Some games are played to prevent anything new happening – these protect the status quo from people like you who want to make changes.

Strategists' checklist

- Ask around to get a better idea of how strategy is developed in your organisation. Find out if it's informal or formal, top down or bottom up.

- Read the existing strategy if it's available to you. Read the annual report.

- Understand the strategic position of your organisation by using the tools in this book.

- Look for opportunities to get involved in any work that is interested in the bigger picture or shaping the future.

- Contribute effectively and your credibility as a strategic thinker will increase. Use your influence to join the strategic conversation.

- Get better at influencing and pitching ideas. Study specific books on the subject.

- Develop a community of people with an interest in shaping the future of the company.

Related ideas

The practical business of selling (and influencing) strategy is neglected in most books on the subject. Yet, the smart strategist can find valuable knowledge in Cialdini's classic book on the psychology of persuasion, *Influence*, and the Heath brothers' book, *Made to Stick*. The important point is a strategy needs to be actively sold as part of a conversation or it will never win enough support to influence an organisation's actions.

two

Thinking like a strategist

To think like a strategist is to see possibilities that can be shaped into situations that are desirable. You have to be able to notice what is happening around you. You should be able to notice historic trends that open up new opportunities. And you need to be able to play a kind of multi-dimensional chess, imagining several moves ahead what your next move should be now.

Events in the real world have many causes. They have so many causes linked in so many weird and wonderful ways that people describe the world as complex and chaotic. There is so much uncertainty, they say, that there is no point making plans or trying to accomplish anything much beyond today.

Skilled strategists *accept* that the world is complex and figure out what to do now to shape events. They do not pretend that they have all of the answers (unless it's helpful to their strategy to pretend), they just look for patterns and then creatively design actions now to shape the future then.

Part of this creative process is instinctive. It is subconscious, relying on natural ability to see and interpret patterns. Yet instinct can be developed and natural talent can be improved upon. You can become better at noticing. You can have insights that lead to new opportunities. And you can get much better at bringing a team together to create ideas and make those ideas happen.

Every page of this strategy book is about thinking and acting like a strategist. The next sub-topics are about particular aspects of this strategic thinking ability. You will learn how reacting is as important as planning. You will gain insights into the value of taking risks that jump the uncertainty gap. You will start to look over your shoulder and look for where the grass is greener.

The strategist's toolkit (on page 163) has been especially devised to help you to think like a strategist. Each tool can be used in a creative or less creative way as you develop your strategic thinking skills. Even the most well-known of the tools, SWOT (page 167) for example, can be used to create remarkable insights into how to find sources of new value that your organisation can deliver.

Take a look at Porter's 5 forces (on page 169) and really think about what those forces mean for your company. Examine Burgelman's strategy dynamics model (page 173) to see how your market and company fit into the rule-keeping and rule-changing continuum. Try out Stacey's uncertainty and agreement model (page 219) to discover whether your company is edging towards chaos or stuck in complacency.

Look at Mintzberg's distinctions between emergent, planned and realised strategy (page 213). The skilled strategist knows that strategy is much more than the plan. You will recognise the bigger picture and start to be able to shape situations through actions now. You will start to think like a strategist. And there's power in that.

Reacting is as important as planning

Successful strategy is often about reacting to events. Planning only takes you so far because you don't know what will happen in the future – you can only guess. The smart strategist allows strategy to be shaped by events. Good reactions can make great strategy.

Frequency: Every problem, every opportunity!
Key participants: First, you. Then, everyone.
Strategy rating: Strategy6

Young Ingvar Kamprad used unexpected cash from his father – a gift for good exam results – to found IKEA. He lived near furniture makers so reacted by selling furniture. He reacted to a boycott from local rivals by producing his own furniture. His first designer reacted to not being able to fit a table in a car by creating the first flat-pack. He reacted to his showroom burning down by building a huge replacement. He reacted to excessive customer demand by starting self-service. The IKEA strategy came from clever reactions to great unplanned opportunities.

Objective

Unplanned opportunities may be your best chance of creating a great strategy so you need to be constantly looking for them. Evidence supports the idea that the most successful entrepreneurs and leaders are fantastic at noticing opportunities. And the greatest opportunities come from reactions to unplanned events. So, ask yourself:

- Does this problem let us start again and do it better?
- What can we do today that was impossible yesterday?
- Is our plan still working? How can we take advantage of events?

Any fool can produce a plan. The genius is in seeing how new events open up new possibilities for the old plan. Or even entirely new plans that weren't possible when the old plan was written. The strategist is continually sifting through events for evidence about how well the plan is working. He wants to see new opportunities for achieving his objectives. Or new objectives that were previously impossible.

Context

Most corporations have an annual planning cycle. They spend some time (usually not enough) thinking about what they want to achieve. They produce a document that lists a series of objectives, priorities and even tasks. The moment the plan is printed it is viewed as complete.

Some people follow the plan. They pretend (or believe) that it's perfect. Some managers insist the plan is followed as a point of principle. The plan demands a response from senior executives, senior managers, managers and professionals. Every level of the hierarchy produces their own version of the master plan – sometimes the process takes nearly a year of cascaded documents. So it's worth asking a few questions:

■ What happens when the assumptions in the plan are wrong?

■ How do employees challenge the assumptions in the plan?

■ By the time the planning is complete, will the plan be out of date?

Other people ignore the plan. They don't read it. And they certainly don't think it has anything to do with the day-to-day of their job. They may react to events but the way that they react seldom changes. They understand the limitations of plans – the contradictions, the ignorance and lack of specific detail – but they don't understand the power of plans to shape responses to events.

The danger is that following the plan too slavishly (without responding to events) will lead the company efficiently in the wrong direction. The right plan can be made wrong by events. The danger of not following any plan is that actions are out of step with each other, may stop any plan working or fail to improve the impact of everyone working together.

Challenge

It's difficult for some people to accept that reacting (not just planning) is a good thing. Managers have been taught the value of being (or looking!) organised. They have learned that being 'proactive' is what the business world wants. They have been told that being reactive is a bad thing. It's good to plan but it's bad to think that you can plan for everything. You need a prepared mind ready to recognise unplanned opportunities.

The good news is that openly discussing the benefits of reacting and the limits of planning is healthy for the business. There is something for everyone in the idea. It can bring together those who believe all plans work and those who believe that the day-to-day is all that matters. Both are right. And wrong.

Another practical challenge is making room for both kinds of strategy in the formal ways that your team or company is organised. Strategy is more effective if it is adapted throughout the year. Some of this is adjustment in the way that the strategy is executed; individual managers and colleagues may figure out how to react to circumstances in order to deliver the official plan.

But some changes to objectives, plans and direction benefit from being brought back into the formal strategy. It's a way of acknowledging that strategy has changed. It's a method for encouraging effort to be focused on new opportunities. It can reduce the negative impact of too many alternative approaches and it's a lot more effective than simply planning, closing your eyes and waiting for the results at the end of the year!

Success

You'll know that you're getting better at reacting (not just planning) when you find that some of the greatest achievements of the past year were not part of the plan at the start of the year.

Your approach to planning will be more fluid. You will include options for moving in other directions if circumstances change. You will examine 'what if' scenarios while planning. You will become smart and fast enough to recognise a fantastic new opportunity (or an awful new threat) while there is time to react intelligently – and know how to use them to better achieve your ambitions.

You will make 'fire-fighting' part of your strategy and you will include more of the people who do the reacting on a day-to-day basis. Middle managers, supervisors and people working at the front line – they can all help to recognise a need for clever reactions to real-world events and circumstances.

Strategists' measures of success

→ You have a way of recognising new unplanned opportunities.

→ You review reactions to problems to see if they should change strategy.

→ Everyone in the business can share reactions and problems with the boss.

→ Your strategy is reviewed and challenged more often than once a year!

→ Reaction times (or responsiveness) are actively improved.

Pitfalls

Reactions to situations can be counterproductive. Unplanned actions can work against the strategy. People can make ad hoc decisions that make sense to them but not to the bigger picture. Or many unplanned actions can make sense individually but not together. The point here is not to encourage excessive chaos. Instead you want channelled initiative and creativity.

Strategists' checklist

■ List things that have gone wrong or problems you have faced. Consider how these problems affect the strategy and the actions to support it.

■ Explore reactions to problems. Figure out whether these ad hoc solutions offer new opportunities to improve the strategy.

■ Use scenario planning approaches to examine possible turning points in the future. It will help you recognise opportunities to react to.

■ Talk to people! Your boss. Your peers. Colleagues at all levels. Particularly the middle and front line of the organisation. They know what is working. They know what is failing and they can tell you while there's still time to react.

■ Take the time to explain to everyone what the strategic direction means to them. It's the best way to make sure that individual reactions support what you're trying to achieve.

Related ideas

Henry Mintzberg argues that there are several different kinds of strategy: *Planned strategy* – what you decide to do; *Realised strategy* – plans that happen the way you expected; and *Emergent strategy* – the unplanned pattern of actions that happen over time (see page 213). Research by Laurent Mirabeau, at the Telfer School of Management in Ottawa, suggests this often happens when people try to do something that is deliberately strategic without formal permission. This kind of autonomous strategic behaviour can lead to emergent strategy – something that endures – or fades away, strategy that is described as 'ephemeral'. A strategic path that could have been.

Taking risks (jump your uncertainty gaps)

All decisions are about the future. Since the future is uncertain, all your decisions will have an uncertain outcome. But because you're trying to shape the future you still need to decide. Part of this is assessing levels of uncertainty. The other part is making decisions that can give you the best chance of succeeding despite uncertainty.

Frequency: When slowed by indecision.
Key participants: You and the team.
Strategy rating: ****

Facing multi-million dollar losses, Lego took the risky decision to hire its new CEO from outside the family. And the new CEO decided to scrap many of the most imaginative projects launched in recent years – risking the innovation culture that had made Lego famous. He increased strategic focus by returning to the essence of Lego – a unified system for creative problem solving. And then took the risky decision to return the power for delivering this strategic vision to his talented team. Working with half the colours, and half the number of components, designers were encouraged to create new toys with what they had – and to work more closely with Lego enthusiasts outside the company. Successfully jumping the uncertainty gap, often by reducing complexity, has transformed Lego into the world's biggest toy company.

Objective

Uncertainty can only be reduced by committed decisions and actions. You can't wait for uncertainty to disappear but you can choose to create certainty of purpose and direction. You can't remove risk but you can think about how to create a culture and processes to adapt to unexpected problems.

- How high are levels of uncertainty in your industry?
- What uncertainty surrounds a particular decision?
- What are the risks in making (or not making) certain decisions?
- How could things go wrong? What would you do next?

People think differently about risk and uncertainty. Managers tend to take fewer gambles than entrepreneurs because of differences between how they view the relative benefits of winning and losing. Small groups tend to take bigger gambles than individuals because they get to share the benefits while also avoiding the blame. But large groups may seek to avoid risks because they get stuck in habitual, traditional ways of doing business.

Avoiding risk is not the main aim of a business. The aim of a business is to take risks and benefit from the higher returns of taking those risks. That's why the entrepreneurial approach to making investments is attractive to growth strategy. And it's why large organisations try to recapture small-group risk taking. They understand doing nothing is often as risky as doing something.

Context

Some risk comes from outside the organisation, but most risk is about the ability of an organisation to complete its plan. The risky part is adapting successfully to the needs and demands of the market. The risk is dealing with competitor moves while managing to deliver products and services that customers will buy. And keeping your shareholders satisfied.

Strategy involves completion of goals, and the risk is the difference between those goals and the ability of the organisation to achieve them. So part of the risk is *created* by the strategy. That means your ability to think about the way various parts of your plan fit together with what your company can do.

- Which risks are outside your direct control?
- Which risks are within your direct control?
- How can you deal with changes outside your control?
- How can you anticipate external changes?

Your task as strategist is to recognise the costs and benefits of risks. The benefits are just as important as the costs. Your strategy will have uncertain outcomes but you can try to assess the rewards and how to gain them.

The next task comes from comparing what you want to accomplish with the abilities and resources available to you. Some of this will be money and equipment but most of it will be the skills, commitment, processes and culture of your company. Part of this will be about the ability to do what is necessary, and part will be the willingness of the organisation to take action that has an uncertain outcome.

Challenge

The first challenge is to look clearly at different sources of risk. As already discussed, some are inside and some of them are outside the organisation.

Outside the organisation	Inside the organisation
▪ Is your market complex or simple?	▪ How demanding are aspirations?
▪ Are the rules of the market stable, dynamic or chaotic?	▪ How high are performance levels?
	▪ Is there a performance/ aspiration gap?
▪ Are resources scarce or plentiful?	▪ How similar is the top team?
▪ Is the market growing or shrinking? How is the general economy doing?	▪ Does the top team have a stake in the business?
	▪ What levels of slack resources exist?
▪ Are there shocks beyond your market?	▪ What skills does the organisation have?

If the gap is large between aspirations and performance levels the risk of not succeeding is increased. If the top team is very similar they may avoid risks because they are comfortable with the status quo. Yet similarity may also increase willingness to take risks if they feel overconfident in their own view of the world. This is not necessarily a good or a bad thing, it depends on the needs of the situation. You should just be aware of team dynamics related to uncertainty so you can respond to it as useful to your objectives.

If the skills are high enough then the capability gap is reduced. This may reduce risk by increasing performance, but it may also increase aspirations to unattainable levels. All of this will affect the risk inherent in the strategy. It is the gap between aspiration and ability that is ultimately the source of risk.

There are various methods some organisations use to analyse risk. These include Net Present Value (NPV) (not covered in this book) where subjective judgements about risk are given numerical values that are subject to a simulation method. Yet the basis of the method is still subjective and does not deal with complex choices.

For complex choices, decision trees have been used. Alternative options and change events are identified alongside likely performance and outcomes. Like NPV these can either be too simple to be accurate or too complex to be useful. They can fool managers into believing they have control over the future. Just as importantly they can stop managers feeling they can intuitively manage the gap between capability and aspiration.

Another approach is scenario planning (see page 183) whereby the strategist uses imagination to 'see' into the future and design actions that can be taken to shape the future. This is about reducing uncertainty by taking certain actions that are under the control of the organisation.

Success

The strategist is attempting to find a course of action that leads to activities which bring attractive results for the organisation and its stakeholders. You are succeeding if you can think your way forward from the current position to a new position that is better. Move from where you are with what you have to where you want to be.

You need to recognise what is in your control and what is outside of your control. You need to get a good understanding of any gap between aspiration and performance. And you need to bridge that gap either by increasing aspiration to the point that people are willing to try to achieve more, or by increasing performance to the point that it can achieve what is desired.

Strategists' measures of success

→ You have identified attractive destinations and objectives.

→ A credible strategy for attaining objectives is created.

→ Level of outside uncertainty is understood.

→ Size of performance/aspiration gap is identified.

→ The capability/uncertainty gap is managed effectively.

Pitfalls

Taking on too much risk happens when you don't have the ability to do what you set out to achieve. People may be overconfident because of past successes or excessively high optimism in world markets. People may take on too much because they either overestimate the ability of colleagues or underestimate the difficulty of the task. This is made worse if a lack of openness or excessive politeness stops people voicing concerns. Defensiveness can lead to ignorance that increases risk.

It is just as much of a problem if ambitious projects and goals are not attempted. The returns to the business will be low and may be too low to keep the business safe. Shareholders may find this unacceptable and the business will not survive if excessive caution loses market share and profit. The task of the strategist and leadership team is to reduce uncertainty in the areas that they can directly influence in order to pursue attractively difficult objectives.

Strategists' checklist

- Identify the areas inside and outside your control.

- Assess levels of uncertainty inside and outside the organisation. Look at the list of questions in this section. Talk about them with your team and think about the likely direction of change. Think about how the organisation can cope with unexpected and expected problems.

- Compare performance aspirations and expectations. If aspirations are greater than expectations consider how to reduce the gap by increasing performance or by reducing aspirations in the short term. If expectations are higher than aspirations then consider how to raise aspirations.

- Use scenario planning tools (see page 183) to consider how strategies may increase or decrease risk in the future. Use the 5 forces model (see page 169) to identify forces that may increase or decrease risks to your competitive position.

- Explore the use of risk analysis and decision-making tools (NPV and Decision Trees). Are they stopping appropriate levels of risk taking? Would they be helpful in improving understanding of risk?

- Think about the capability of the company to do what is required by the strategy. Consider also the ability of culture and skills to adapt to unforeseen problems, particularly if the strategy is ambitious.

Related ideas

Nassim Taleb, in his book *The Black Swan*, argues that people have an inaccurate view of risk. This means that they take on risk that they underestimate and avoid risk that they overestimate. This is exacerbated by lack of information, personal fears and group dynamics.

Being aware of these tendencies can help you to take the kind of actions that your competitors fear to attempt while in fact not taking foolish risks. This is what entrepreneurs do instinctively as they demonstrate a form of functional impulsiveness along with superior pattern-recognition skills.

Unfortunately, many organisations find it easier to be managerial than entrepreneurial. Managers may keep investing in continual improvement efforts that continually fail. They may also abandon investments in more radical innovation, even when there is more risk in moving slowly than moving too quickly.

Yet, according to research led by Sucheta Nadkarni at Cambridge Judge Business School, when new opportunities are appearing, and disappearing at high speed, you will often be rewarded for competitive aggressiveness. In such environments, strategic urgency helps you to adapt so that you get to the future in time.

Looking over your shoulder

Strategies compete with strategies. Organisations compete with other organisations. You need to be aware of what the competition is doing. You need to know what customers are doing. Paranoid adaptation is part of the strategy game. Look up, down, back and ahead.

Frequency: Regularly.
Key participants: You.
Strategy rating: ***

Netflix – the internet streaming media company – has been driven by a passionate desire to try new things. They know that someone somewhere is doing something that will threaten their survival. So they are willing to cannibalise their own business. They were called 'a worthless piece of crap' by analysts who thought competitors would catch up. So they moved faster. With more than 60 million subscribers in over 40 countries, original TV series and movies winning Emmys and Oscars, Netflix uses criticism to motivate constant reinvention of their wildly successful strategy.

Objective

Strategy should not be created in a vacuum because strategy cannot be executed (made to work) in a vacuum. Competitive strategy works in a context created by the actions (and likely actions) of the competition. It's surprising how often leaders do not know what their competition is doing or why.

- What is your competition doing?
- What are the best companies in the world doing?
- What are others companies doing better than you?

These questions are a good starting point. You should shop in your competitors' shops. You should buy your competitors' products and use their services. Spend time in their space. Get a constant stream of ideas from the competition so you can learn from them and figure out what they do better than you. Or what the best in the world are doing. The best ideas in the world are not in your head, your organisation or your industry. So look around.

Don't be obsessed with copying the competition, but do learn from them. You can choose to adapt what you find, or do the complete opposite as a way of differentiating your own strategy. You can combine ideas from different competitors and create something new.

Context

Make your competition seem real. Bring them to life. Real, living, breathing people who are trying to do better than you. Smart people who are moving faster than you. Create a competition wall. Stick their logos up. Pin up their products. Enlarge criticisms – even the insults. Use it to motivate creativity.

The ex-CEO of BlackBerry used to put his own product in the centre of the room during meetings. The idea was to talk about how to improve the value of what was offered to customers. Unfortunately, it also blinded them to external competition and innovation. They were stuck inside the limits of their product traditions. It's better to have the very best of your competitors' products surrounding yours – challenging you to do better.

- What would you do to improve your competitors' products?
- What is the secret of your success?
- What could the competition do to wipe you out?
- How would you respond to the worse/best your competition could do?

When you find something you can do easily, that's great. But be really interested when you find something that would be hard to do. It might be hard because of technical or practical difficulties. Or hard to do because it would destroy businesses (or revenue) that you already have. But that's what makes it attractive as a strategy. It won't be easy for the competition either.

Challenge

It's hard for many people to focus on anything outside of their immediate surroundings. They are paid to pay attention to the tasks that go along with their job description. Working days are full of the way things are done around here. Meetings are used to review progress against projects. Objectives tend to ignore what is happening right now – and what might happen next.

It's not easy to look around. There isn't much time, and a lot of what you might see will create more work, and decisions, or arguments about where to go and what to do.

Managers sometimes survive by *not* questioning the status quo. And yet strategy benefits from being able to reverse assumptions. It is helped by looking outside to find competitor actions that justify improvements.

Even if you spend the time to look around, a few challenges remain. You'll need to make decisions (or influence someone else to make them) to go after the competition. You'll have to create positive action from paranoia. And you'll have to avoid the kind of me-too copying that puts you in a worse position.

- Who are your competitors?
- Which competitors motivate you?
- Who is doing the best work in your industry?
- Who is doing the best, most exciting work in any industry?

It's important to choose competitors carefully. They can inspire you to do better. They can show you what is possible. They can give you that child-like love of improvement. They can show you how to do what you really need to do and give you a reason for doing it.

Success

You'll know that you're getting better at looking over your shoulder (at the competition) when your sense of urgency increases. Instead of watching the clock – to see how much longer the day will be – you will watch the competition to see how much longer you have before they catch up.

Our work has the meaning that we give to it. Your work can mean more when you do your job in a way that competes with the other people in the race. It's more fun if you are trying to do better than the people in other companies who care about the same things that you do.

When you look around you'll know what threats are coming before they do serious damage. You will understand more about what makes competitors successful and about what may make them more dangerous in the future. You won't fall into the trap of dismissing new entrants just because they're new, or underestimate traditional players just because they're old.

Strategists' measures of success

→ You have a list of threats and dangers.

→ You create a competitor wall (or something similar) to keep them real.

→ Everyone in the business spends time using and reviewing competitor products.

→ You recognise strategic turning points for your organisation and industry.

→ A sense of urgency (and passion) is increased as you try to run faster.

Pitfalls

It's important not to obsess about the competition if it stops you doing great work. People are different. Some will be motivated by what the competition is doing and what might happen next; others will worry about things they can't change or feel bad about what you do. Encourage pride in all the good things that you do. Protect people from real paranoia. It's your job as a leader to look over your shoulder every now and then – often enough to re-energise your team and avoid danger.

Strategists' checklist

- List the great (and bad) things that your competition is doing. Understand how they do what they do well enough to respond to them.

- List the great things that people in other industries are doing. Who are your inspirations? What products do you buy? Who do you admire?

- Make the competition real. Create a mannequin of a key rival. Buy their products and make a product table for people to try. Make a wall of competitor adverts, services, especially their criticisms of you.

- Have short meetings to look over your shoulder. Have long meetings using scenarios. Explore how you can respond to the best work of your competitors. Think about how to react to opportunities.

Related ideas

Andy Grove – ex-CEO of Intel – wrote the book *Only the Paranoid Survive*. He argues that strategy must respond to inevitable changes in the competitive landscape by displaying a kind of paranoid flexibility. This approach allows you to survive by taking smart actions at strategic inflection points and turning them into opportunities to shape the future (see page 173). Such a high adaptability approach is particularly important given what Richard D'Aveni, Giovanni Dagnino and Ken Smith refer to as an 'age of temporary advantage'. Ask yourself, as they suggest, what happens when there are no sustainable competitive advantages?

Knowing where the grass (really) is greener

It's a fair bet that at some point what made your company money in the past will stop making money. New products replace old products. Entirely new services will replace old services. The best places to sell your products will change. And the customers who mattered so much will stop (or start) buying. You need to know when (and how) to switch focus.

Frequency: Quarterly, regularly.
Key participants: Leadership teams.
Strategy rating: ****

Intel made billions by successfully dominating the desktop computer market in the USA. The grass has been green on their side of the fence but there are now more people using the internet on mobile devices than on desktop computers. There are more people using those mobile devices in the rest of the world than the traditional richest nations. And the internet of things, connecting everything from robots to security to your self-driving car, will soon be bigger than the internet of people. Intel knows that the next big thing *is* coming. It knows that the grass is *greener* on the other side. You need to know when that's true for your company, so you know when to move your focus to new markets.

Objective

Knowing when to focus on new markets is a very important part of competitive strategy. Often it's a big-picture issue – not something that should surprise you. It shouldn't be an unplanned opportunity because you should be able to see this kind of market movement ahead of time. And it shouldn't really be about reacting (see page 27) because it's often about long-term trends.

- Is your existing market growing, stagnating or shrinking?
- Are levels of competition growing, stable or shrinking?
- Where are the markets that are growing faster than yours?

If your market is growing fast enough to suit everyone, then your grass is green enough, but a market decline is going to cause you problems. Even market stagnation will require changes eventually, and if your competition grows into new markets, they will come back with new resources that may threaten you.

Context

If your market continues to grow, then it will give new opportunities in the future for expansion. As a strategic thinker you will want to have ideas about when and where to expand.

It could be that your market is growing fast enough but your competition is growing even faster. The end result could still become a real problem for your company. A relatively small decrease in market share can have a big impact on your levels of profitability, and your competitors can use that market share to drive their own expansion in a cycle of growth that is, again, potentially damaging to your company.

Be particularly aware of new competitors. These are people who have noticed something about your market that is attractive. They may have come from other markets in search of 'greener grass'. They may have spotted opportunities to do something amazing that you haven't seen yet.

Any market growing faster than yours is worth looking at carefully. A strategic decision to enter a fast-growing market is worth considering. It could be a market that is small but that will be bigger than yours eventually, or a market that is big but still growing. It could be a market which is similar to yours, or a segment of an existing market, or a market that is extremely different but could be pursued by investing profits from your existing markets.

Challenge

It's hard for some people to sacrifice what they have now (the green grass) for what *might* be on the other side of the fence. If they have enjoyed success in the existing market then they will take some convincing that the time has come to explore new markets. You will need to provide a strong argument.

■ How fast is the new market growing?

■ What will happen if you ignore new markets?

Part of being a strategic thinker is becoming a strategic presenter (see page 20). You should be considering the strongest statistics and trends on different sides of the case for new markets. The important thing is to be able to clarify the situation so that the best (not perfect) decision can be made.

■ Where is the new market growing? What is the geography of growth?

■ What demographics are driving the growth?

■ Who are the main competitors in the new market?

■ Which consumer trends are most important to the new market?

Understanding the new market opportunity is important, but understanding how to make the new market work for your company is more important. The next step is to explore the recipe for success and consider how to take advantage of the new market.

■ Do you have what it takes to win in the new market?

■ What would it take to acquire the right skills and knowledge?

■ How do you focus on two markets at once?

Success

Knowing your own market is the start. You'll know its size, your market share and your advantages, and you'll know the same for your competitors. You will know whether you are being squeezed between competitive forces. You will know how that might happen in the future. You'll understand the key trends in your market and how they may alter the attractiveness of your position.

Your company will also know about a range of other markets. You will know which are closest to you: their size, growth, demographics and key trends. You will also be aware of the fastest-growing markets in other industries. Growth may offer opportunity and threat. The fastest growth areas are most likely to have an impact on seemingly non-related industries.

You will know what it takes to compete and what it would take to move into new markets, and your company will have a better understanding of the decision points in the future. When will it make sense to enter new markets?

Strategists' measures of success

→ You know whether (and how much) your market is growing or shrinking.

→ Sources (and levels) of competition in your market are known.

→ Fast-growing markets have been identified and explored.

→ Strong arguments and plans for moving into new markets are ready.

→ Leadership (in particular) is ready to invest and move as necessary.

Pitfalls

You may fail. Not all fast-growing markets will be suitable for the experience your company can offer. You may see the opportunity. Everyone may agree that something has to change, but that doesn't mean you know *how*. You may lack the strategic resources (see page 177) or the knowledge or the processes or the relationships to make the journey. Every new market has barriers to entry.

Alternatively, forecasts for the new market may simply be too optimistic. They may change quickly. Perhaps growth is less than anticipated, or there is a stampede of new competitors who have seen what you have seen. The result will be lower margins and profits than you thought.

Strategists' checklist

▪ Examine the likely growth of your existing market. Consider what this will mean for your company in the future. Think about what your company can do strategically to achieve its objectives if the market slowed down.

▪ Explore alternative fast-growing markets. Start with those closest to your existing products and services. Then think about the fastest growing markets in the world. Look at how existing products could be sold to new markets. Look at how you could develop new products.

▪ Make sure the opportunities are real. It's important not to run away from hard work (or hard decisions) in your existing market. You may find that your new market is much harder than the one you left behind.

▪ Make sure that you know the cost of doing nothing (or staying in your existing market). Even if the new market is tough it may be worth experimenting. There are risks to changing *and* to not changing.

Related ideas

Michael Porter identifies five forces that change where the grass is greenest: *Existing Competitors* – how well they compete; *New Entrants* – increased competition because more people competing; *Substitutes* – reduced because people don't need what you do; *Suppliers* – who make life easier or harder depending on demand and supply for their products; and *Buyers* – whose demand for your products depends on their income and interest (see page 169). What you do in response to those five forces is about the psychology of behavioural strategy. This includes, as Thomas Powell points out, the rationality of economics (reductionism), the politics of groups (pluralism) and the mindsets of individuals (contextualism).

three

Creating your strategy

At some point, you will want to create your strategy for getting from where you are to where you would like to be. Even if you are entirely happy where you are, you will still need a strategy for keeping yourself there. Other people are creating strategies and making waves that may change your situation.

Part of creating strategy is seeing the bigger picture. You want to take the time to see beyond the immediate tasks of the day, and if you take that time you can see your tasks in the context of the market or overall situation. You can definitely act without knowing where you are, but it helps if you can shape your actions to the situation you're in. And that's where strategy helps.

Within the bigger picture, you will be looking for where you want to go – your desired position. Your strategy will have an overall strategic intention and direction. Use the key strategy questions to find a direction that delivers what you really want to accomplish.

Creating strategy is also about finding advantages – discovering something you can do that makes what you do worthwhile or profitable. You can actively look for overlap between what you want to contribute and what the business says it wants to accomplish.

You can create strategy that allows you to do something the world wants while surviving and thriving in business. Value and profit are not automatically the same thing. Strategy allows you to consider the difference between the overall impact of actions and the narrow pursuit of short-term business goals. It's important not to win the quarter and lose the decade.

The strategy you create is never complete. It is a living set of answers to the basic, powerful strategy questions. You will need to react to events and adapt to competitors if the overall intentions of the group are to be realised in productive ways.

You will have to make strategic decisions about what to do about the bigger picture. You don't have to decide everything but there are certain decisions that are helpful to your success. There are decisions that will focus your people on achieving a particular objective. And there are smart decisions that leave you ready to do new great things in the future.

Seeing the big picture?

Strategists think about the big picture. They consider more than
the list of things to do, or the production schedule, or the plan for
the next few months. Strategists are interested in the long term –
what's going to happen in a year, decade and century. They are also
interested in things that are happening outside of their company,
country and industry.

Frequency: Regularly. Take some time out.
Key participants: You and your boss.
Strategy rating: ****

The idea for Twitter came from a big-picture brainstorming day.
Employees from a podcasting company spent time thinking
about strategy and how to survive when faced with tough
competition from Apple. One came up with an idea for an
SMS service. The company decided to prototype it and later
the group bought the company. Ten years later they have over
300 million users and a 20 billion dollar valuation. Twitter's
success came from looking beyond the existing plan.

Objective

Considering the big picture (and what to do about it) is an essential part of strategy. It is the essence of being a strategic thinker
to be able to look up from the day-to-day and really see other
opportunities.

Getting the day-to-day work done may turn out to be a lot less
important to you and your company than it seems today. There
may be dangers in the bigger picture that will make what you are
doing a waste of time. There may be opportunities that make your
existing goals relatively unimportant.

Look forward

Exploring the future is one part of the bigger picture. What is likely to happen to your company if current trends continue? What happens if current assumptions are wrong? How long can you last if a key market disappears? What great things could happen if you change direction?

The purpose of looking forward is to judge when it's better to change. If you look forward you can take advantage of opportunities in the future. You can better understand the implications of events today if you have a future context – a bigger picture – against which to understand them.

Look backwards

Thinking about the past is another part of the big picture. Where did the success of the company come from? What has worked since the company started? What has failed? What projects have been attempted? How has the past led to the situation the company is in now? What lessons can be learned? What lessons need to be unlearned?

The purpose of looking backwards is to understand better the reasons that the company is the way it is and is doing what it is doing. It is easier to see trends over time. It is also easier to understand people's positions and perspectives if you know what has happened in the life of the company.

Look outwards

Shifting your attention outside of your company, market or country is an important part of the big picture. What are the fastest growing trends in the world? What social changes could have an impact on your company? What are competitors doing? What are the new normal ways of doing things? Are you being left behind? Who can you learn from?

The purpose of looking outwards is to see what other people are missing. You should be reading magazines and articles from other industries. You should experiment with technologies that are nothing to do with your job. It's a good idea to travel, to take photos and to get curious about the outside world.

Context

While at work, many people limit their view of the world to the job they do and the team that they are in. This is the smaller picture. They don't see how what they do contributes to the rest of the business. They don't see how they could change what they do to help other parts of the business. And they don't see the threats to their job from changes that are part of the bigger picture. So it's worth asking some questions:

- What is the official (or formal) strategy of the business?
- How well is the company and industry doing?
- What are other people saying about your company and industry?
- How does your job (and the work of your team) contribute?

There are many other questions you could be asking. The important thing is that you consider the bigger picture so that you can make better decisions and take more effective actions. If you don't consider the bigger picture, you're not thinking like a strategist (see Part 2) and you're not going to be able to take advantage of opportunities or avoid threats that are coming your way.

Challenge

It's important to look forward, backwards and outside your company as part of seeing the big picture, but it's only the start. The next step is to simplify the various details into a big picture that helps you understand what is happening.

This simplified model of the world also makes it easier for other people to see the big picture. If they see the big picture as a simple model, you can discuss what should happen next with less confusion. You can plan strategy with a clearer understanding of how your actions are meant to shape the future, and you can get support for your strategic ideas because people have a clear idea of your arguments.

It is worth emphasising that the big picture should be represented visually – it should be a big picture of the business and its place in the world. Seeing the big picture is about looking carefully at events and possibilities, but sharing the big picture is much easier if it is graphical. This is one of the reasons for the enduring popularity of the best models featured in this book (see Part Six: *The Strategy Book* toolkit).

Success

You'll know that you're getting better at seeing the bigger picture when you can fit new pieces of information into your mental big picture of the business. You'll read about an event and know how that is likely to impact the existing (and future) plans of the business. And you'll start to recognise opportunities because you become skilled at imagining different scenarios.

You will also be able to draw simple pictures representing your business. It doesn't have to be beautiful, just a functional diagram that shows how your business works and the pressures, threats and opportunities it faces. It is important that you can communicate your version of the bigger picture with others to get support.

You will be known as someone who sees the bigger picture, and, just as importantly, you will be able to apply these ideas to the political climate so that you can recognise the best ways of influencing others. The strategic thinker should be able to apply these ideas to personal and business ambitions.

Strategists' measures of success

→ Everyone has a bigger picture view of the future.

→ Your company has a big-picture sense of where success has come from.

→ The work you do fits into a big-picture view of company and industry.

→ You have simplified the big picture so it helps to clarify choices.

Pitfalls

Looking at the bigger picture can get complicated. There can be so many things to consider that you don't know what to do, or even what is really going on. That's why it is so important that you use the tools in this book to simplify the bigger picture. A strategist cannot get lost in the detail, you need to rise above it and so make sense of the bird's eye view. You have to provide a clear map that helps others to understand the big picture and do something about it.

Strategists' checklist

- Find out about the formal mission and strategy of your organisation (see page 223).

- Think about how your role contributes to your company's success.

- Use SWOT (page 167), the 5 forces (page 169) and scenario planning (page 183) to better understand the big picture and have something to share with colleagues.

- Examine the future, past and present to look for parts of the big picture that affect your organisation.

- Bring them together into a diagram or sketch that shows how your business works and how that might change in the future.

- Identify key trends and events. Discuss regularly with your team.

Related ideas

Clayton Christensen argues in *The Innovator's Dilemma* that many companies that listen to their best customers and work to build new products for them are blinded to the bigger picture. Success from doing what you are doing stops you seeing what you should do next. This is a bias, towards habit-based inertia, that is explored in *The Innovation Book*.

Finding position, intention and direction

It's important to know the answers to several questions: Where are you going to compete in relation to your competitors? What do you intend achieving as a part of the bigger picture? And from where you are, what direction do you want to follow, and at what speed?

Frequency: Annually with regular review.
Key participants: Top team *with* organisation.
Strategy rating: Strategy6

Apple was in decline. It was bereft of ideas and confused about its position in the market. It was building grey, ugly computers and trying to sell them at twice the price of Windows PCs. Steve Jobs - one of its founders - returned and that helped. Jonathon Ives - an industrial designer - designed the candy coloured iMac and that helped. But it was only after the serendipitous success of the iPod that Apple was able to develop a distinctive strategic position complete with iPhone, iPad and Apple Watch. Now, with Tim Cook in charge, Apple has become the world's most valuable company.

Objective

It is helpful to know what you are trying to do. This includes determining specific goals and individual tasks to be completed. But strategy is about connected, cumulative tasks that are worth more than the sum of their parts. The value of individual actions is relative to the actions of competitors and the needs of consumers.

People who work with you want to know how you fit into their view of the market. Customers who buy your products and services also need to get a sense of how your products compare distinctively to those offered by the competition. Your colleagues need to know what you're trying to achieve (and not achieve) so that they can contribute effectively.

Choosing a strategic position that is distinct can also help you to avoid direct, counterproductive competition, but only if that position is different enough to stop the competition from coming back at you too quickly. In the Apple example, they managed to create a combination of product and service features that proved very difficult to copy years after they established the original position.

Context

Part of finding a position is about knowing what you want to achieve and stating it in a way that everyone (or most people) can understand. That's the orientation part of strategy, letting people know where they stand in relation to where you want the company to go.

Statements of mission and purpose have gained a bad reputation, but that's only because of all the times that they are created without a meaningful link to what the company really wants to do. They are meaningless, and worse – they disappoint the people who work for the organisation.

And yet the mission statement (like the one-page strategy – see page 142) can be a powerful rallying call. It can allow subsequent decisions and actions to be judged against the overall strategic intention. Apple's mission statement is one paragraph and includes the following statements:

- Apple designs the *best* personal computers in the world.
- Apple *leads* the digital music revolution.
- Apple *reinvented* the mobile phone with its *revolutionary* iPhone and App store.
- Apple introduced its *magical* iPad which is defining the future of mobile.

The mission statement is a kind of strategy history. It shows direction from the initial intention to design 'the best' personal computers to leading the digital revolution. And then how the mobile phone was reinvented, leading to the current strategic intention to define the future of mobile with its magical iPad.

The best mission statements of intention change over time, but they define the positioning, intention and direction of the organisation. They provide clarity to employees, partners and investors. Customers may also be offered a shortened version.

Apple has used the slogan 'This changes everything, again' for a new version of its iPhone and 'Magical and revolutionary device at an unbelievable price' for its original iPad. This kind of coherence helps strategy to succeed.

Challenge

Finding a strategic position is about more than a mission statement. The challenge is to understand the combination of characteristics you offer to customers. Apple designs the 'best computers' and 'revolutionary, magical devices' while Dell intends being the 'Most successful computer company in the world at delivering the best customer experience in markets we serve'.

The two offer very different strategic positions based on very different priorities. Apple competes by designing the best devices while Dell competes by delivering the best customer experience. Apple seeks to be the best in the world while Dell wants to be the most successful in the world and the best in the markets it serves.

If you are a new employee at Dell, you should know that the company is first interested in financial success and market share *ahead* of design, and that it wants a customer experience that exceeds its nearest competitors. It doesn't prioritise having the best technology, best design or magical experiences.

The Apple strategy may lead to greater financial success but that's not the positioning that they have chosen. The Dell strategy may lead to magical design but that's not the strategic intent behind their corporate actions.

The logic and likely consequences of each strategy and statement will influence the actions of employees, partners and customers. And that's why it's worth considering carefully (and creatively) their wording and intention.

Success

You should choose a couple of key characteristics for your brand (and organisation). Apple chose 'design' and 'leadership'. If Dell compared itself with those characteristics, it would put design and leadership as a low priority. Dell is more interested in financial success and relative customer experience. Your key characteristics should allow you to measure your success and compare yourself to others in similar markets (see page 98).

The positioning needs to orient people in the business (see page 195) so that they know which way they are facing, and in what direction they are going to travel. It also needs to be animating so that they are motivated to make a creative, engaged effort and to make that effort in ways that help the organisation.

You will know the key characteristics that will guide your efforts and strategic direction. They may be high price and low quality, or magical design and high brand value, or high fashion and medium quality. There are countless ways to compete in terms of positioning so a complete list can't be offered. The important thing is to have considered the key industry characteristics and *then* consider which additional *unique* characteristics you want to make your own.

From this information, you can build up a strategic positioning map. You can show where your organisation is compared to others in the market, and you can show graphically where your organisation wants to be in the future.

As an example, Dell used to offer medium-quality design at medium prices. They had low-design competitors with lower prices and competitors, like Apple, with high prices for high-quality luxury design. They had to decide whether to defend the middle, move to better design or lower their costs. In the end, they decided to create niche brands for cheapest cost and luxury design. Genius can be doing both.

Twitter lists its mission as 'a work in progress', yet its company slogan is 'the best place to find out what's happening right now', which is a very clear statement of strategic intent (see pages 51 and 191). Facebook, a key competitor, lists its mission as 'giving people the power to share', which is, again, distinct from Twitter.

Ideally, your efforts at positioning will make it simpler to decide what actions fit your strategy, and when you should (or shouldn't) do something. It should influence the style in which things are done. And it should help to guide the efforts of individuals and groups. In this way, people can work with more autonomy within the guiding position, intention and direction of the strategy.

Strategists' measures of success

→ You have figured out the position of the company relative to its market.

→ The intention and focus of the company's actions is specified.

→ Everyone (pretty much) knows where the company is headed – its direction.

→ You have a clear way of communicating position, intention and direction.

→ You have looked at whether the strategy is credible, coherent and motivational enough to get real support and momentum for action.

Pitfalls

Strategic positioning seems like a simple enough task, until you try to create a position that is distinctive. It's easy to end up with a position that is unclear. It's easy to confuse the statement with the position with the slogan. It's also easy enough to create statements that can be understood in very different ways, leading to wasted or counterproductive effort.

For example, when Microsoft talk of 'empowering every person and every organisation on the planet to achieve more', is it immediately apparent what they mean? And if it's not clear then how does it contribute to the strategic coherence of actions? It can be turned into something meaningful, but that takes effort. If you just pay lip service to fancy-sounding statements you will confuse instead of clarifying (see page 142 on managing change).

Strategists' checklist

■ Carefully (and creatively) look at your position in your market. Start from a broad view of what your market includes. Think about the characteristics which are different in the market. Start with cost and quality. Expand into other differences that matter.

■ Plot where you fit on a strategy positioning map. Are you low cost, low quality? Or high cost, high quality? Or have you figured out a way of delivering low cost and high quality? (See page 62 on advantages.)

■ Think about how to clearly state positioning and intentions in the market. Write it down in a one-line slogan. Make sure that comes from a one-paragraph version that reflects historic direction. This helps engage talent within the business.

Related ideas

Michael Porter, Harvard Business Professor, claims positioning is pretty much everything in strategy. Once you know where you want to compete all decisions and actions flow from there. He provided a framework of generic strategies to help make those decisions. But you will need other tools to differentiate in ways that allow success (see page 163).

Sometimes, strategists really do take the planned path by finding the resources they need to cause the position they want. But just as often, argues Saras Sarasvathy, professor at the Indian Institute of Management, entrepreneurial strategists use the resources they have to craft the desirable effects that are possible.

Looking for advantages

Following the rules of your industry will only get you so far. If you keep making products or delivering services just like all your competitors at a price that customers will pay then that's something. But for a creative strategist that isn't enough. You want to find an edge, a competitive advantage that will allow you to make more profit, and grow your business.

Frequency: Formal quarterly, informal continually.
Key participants: You and your organisation.
Strategy rating: **

Aldi, the global supermarket from Germany, believes everything can be cheaper, simpler and better. And they act rigorously on their beliefs – what they call asceticism – by making things cheaper, simpler and better. They sell their own brands wherever possible rather than big brands. Not both. They don't bother customers with coupons and special offers. Just low prices. All employees are involved in continuous improvement. Each store has only three different jobs, forklift driver, cashier and, sometimes, security guard. They want the shopping to be as simple, easy and quick as possible. Up until now, Aldi has grown because of the long-term advantages of strategic simplicity and clarity.

Objective

The aim is to find a set of competitive advantages that allows you to first to survive and then to thrive. There are many different advantages in practice, but there are three generic strategies that are worth discussing as a starting point (see page 171).

Cost leadership means that you can produce the goods or service at a lower cost than any other competitor. You may even share cost leadership with a few close competitors if there is enough competition in the market. For example, a country may be the lowest-cost location for a particular item but there may be several different competitors within that country. There is rarely one cost leader in all areas but the generic strategy is still a good starting point.

You may achieve your cost leadership by being more efficient than other competitors. This efficiency may be achieved by better processes, or manufacturing techniques, or less wasteful quality management. Or low costs may be accomplished by using cheaper labour or by locating closer to the target market and reducing transportation or retail costs.

Differentiation means that you can produce goods or a service that is different to those of your competitors. No one else sells it so you don't have to worry about keeping your costs lower than the competition. You may be able to raise your prices because the differences between your products are so valued by your customers that they will pay the difference. This improvement in demand elasticity has great benefits for your competitive position.

You can be different in an infinite number of ways. Your product can be smaller, bigger, faster, slower, heavier, lighter, uglier or more beautiful. It can fit together with other products in a more pleasing way. It can be promoted by celebrities or amazing viral advertising. It can be more convenient or more prestigious. It can come in different colours and patterns. It can be more efficient, quieter or have any number of new functions.

The point about differentiation is that it has to be valued by the customer more than competing demands for their money and time. And be of more value than it costs you to produce it, allowing you to make a profit to keep making the product or delivering the service. Differentiation is about adjectives and it's judged by whoever is paying you.

Focus is the third generic strategy. In a sense it's a form of differentiation because it's about focusing on a narrow part of a market and keeping other competitors away from that market. This may be because of natural geographic constraints – such as being the only hairdresser in your area.

More often focus is achieved because you differentiate in *who* you target by building advertising and fulfilment processes around those niche customers. And in the long run, you start to make further changes to the service or the product to better meet the needs and aspirations of your niche.

Context

In theory, you can only pick one of the three generic strategies. In practice, the three generic strategies overlap and can be combined.

When there is a significant difference in the cost of production, it can be used to powerful effect. This is particularly true where that significant difference cannot be matched in the short or medium term.

Japanese car manufacturers became many times more cost efficient than their Western rivals. Cost leadership allowed them to undercut their rivals and win market share. Cost leadership also allowed them to match the prices of their rivals and win much greater profit margins that they were then able to invest back into their businesses. This investment made them more competitive in a cycle that was virtuous for Japan and challenging for the West.

By combining generic strategies, Japanese car manufacturers were able to start with low-priced cars aimed at a small car niche and then work their way up into different, more expensive, car categories. They moved up to mid-range family cars, then executive cars, luxury brands, sports cars and finally super-cars to rival Ferrari.

The success of the Japanese was based on competitive advantages of cost leadership focused on particular market segments that turned into differentiation through innovation. And the combination of all three over time established them as hugely successful global corporations.

Challenge

Each of the generic strategies (cost, differentiation and focus) requires various skills to create on paper and to deliver operationally (see page 182). It is one thing to say that you want to be a cost leader, or that having a unique proposition would be helpful. It's quite another to reduce costs beneath your best competitors or find a package of features that customers value as unique and worth paying more to use.

Cost leadership is partly about returns on investment. You showing that your strategy (on paper and operationally) returns more to investors than an alternative strategy. If you can demonstrate the superior returns of money invested in your strategy then you will receive the resources your strategy needs. This is already a form of success since it reduces the resources available to competing strategies at your company and elsewhere. It is success that can build over time so that alternatives and competitors find it harder and harder to obtain investment while your investments grow and reinforce your strategy.

The other – more obvious – part of cost leadership is operationally delivering your product or service at less than your competitors. This requires cost reduction strategy and cost management. You will need to figure out where to source materials, which partners to work with, what production techniques to use and have a very accurate, disciplined supply chain. All this is necessary to deliver cost as a competitive advantage over the long term.

In addition, you will have to consider scales of scale (how much of one item to produce) and scales of scope (how many similar items to produce). These are both traditional ways of reducing costs. Yet innovative techniques like Just In Time (JIT), lean management, Six Sigma, total quality management (TQM), business process re-engineering (BPR) and continuous improvement are other ways of achieving the same aims.

You need to be creative and disciplined. Consult with experts in cost reduction, but also consider a range of alternative ways of achieving the same aims. Zara, for example, produce their clothes locally to their markets in Europe and maintain that they benefit from lower overall costs and greater flexibility than their rivals. As a strategist you have to see the bigger picture (see page 51) and weigh up various (sometimes) conflicting objectives and contradictions.

Marketing is an area which can benefit from scale because the costs of a campaign and media spend are divided by the overall sales of a product. Research and development is another area that can benefit, along with procurement of goods, services and raw materials owing to scale and bargaining power. These indivisibilities are all reasons to support scale as part of a strategy to achieve (and maintain) cost leadership.

Another indivisible strength of scale is that once you have gained the capability or experience to build a product or deliver a service, that capability becomes a core competence that can be used over and over again without increasing its costs. It is the benefit Apple has gained, for example, from only releasing one or two new iPhones at a time. The lessons are learned once and applied to one product which is produced and sold tens of millions of times without increasing costs. Competitors – like Samsung – have many more products. They must divide their expertise and research efforts between all their products. This increases costs. There is tension between focus, segmentation and experimentation.

'Differentiation' involves some kind of unique offer. You are trying to find something about any feature of your product or service that makes it different and more valuable than competing products. You may even find something that makes it impossible for anyone to compete directly.

The challenge is first one of imagination. To differentiate your product at all requires creativity to imagine differences that are possible and even those that are not currently possible. This may require a range of creativity techniques, external perspectives and various kinds of expertise. Next you have to be able to imagine them making a difference that is valued by the customer enough to pay for that difference.

You may find that the differences are not attractive enough to justify the additional costs of delivering them. Or you may find that novelty is not appreciated. It may even be feared or viewed as a negative attribute of your offer to the marketplace.

If the differences are not obviously better from a customer's point of view then there will be costs involved in trying to change minds through marketing – and that takes time with no certainty of success.

The reputation of your company and perception of your brand may also become a differentiator. That may be as simple as trust, or customer service, or added extras that make it worthwhile working with you. Every loyalty scheme and advertising campaign is a way of trying to differentiate.

This is a mixture of tangible and intangible characteristics. And if you get it right, people will buy your product in preference to someone else's because it makes them feel better to be associated with your brand, or because it is more enjoyable to deal with your company.

Success

Understanding the sources of competitive advantage is a starting point. It really helps you to make decisions and create effective strategy if you are able to use the generic strategies as a tool. They can be used creatively to clarify the current position. You can examine alternative strategic moves to see how they would affect your cost, differentiation and focus intentions.

Your strategy should make it clear how the overall intention is translated into competitive advantage. It is one thing to say you will be the best in the world in a certain industry, it's quite another to explain how this is reflected in cost, differentiation and focus.

It is even more powerful if you can use scenarios and strategic games to show how attaining certain advantages will create a virtuous circle or path of competitive advantage. This is real strategic thinking, when consequences are thought through to deliver new possibilities at each stage.

Ideally, you will figure out competitive advantages that have direct benefits for customer groups that are valued (much) more than they cost you to deliver. You will identify a place to compete that is less competitive either because it is uncontested or because your strategy will differentiate you so much that competitors are unable to compete. You want to find something that gives you enough time to build a chain of competitive advantages.

Strategists' measures of success

→ Identify how you compare in cost, differentiation and focus.

→ Find new ways of competing in these three generic areas.

→ Consider how these sources of competitive advantage can be combined.

→ Seek to create virtuous circles or chains of advantages that create new opportunities for you that are difficult for competitors to imitate.

→ Find ways of protecting your advantages.

Pitfalls

You may find that other competitors are already trying to differentiate but are doing it better. Your efforts may cost too much to be worthwhile. Customers may not be as impressed by your differentiation as you were. Your efforts to control costs may be undermined by events, circumstances, technological failures or competitor advances.

You need to make sure that the company is not over reliant on any one attempt to gain a single competitive advantage. There must be adaptability so that you can react to setbacks without losing the company. Most business is based on compromise and multiple Plan B scenarios that let you keep working on various sources of competitive advantage.

The ability to execute your strategy matters more than ever when you are investing resources that only pay off if you become the lowest cost or most unique product or service.

Strategists' checklist

■ Consider what you offer to the marketplace. Are there any competitive advantages? Are any of those long-term advantages?

■ Examine the advantages of other players in the market. How do they compare in costs? Is there anyone who appears to be a cost leader? How do they compare in differentiation? Are you pretty much the same or is someone different enough that they can charge more for their product?

■ Creatively explore how you could deliver competitive advantage in each of the three generic areas. How could you reduce your costs? How could you deliver something valuable that differentiates you and allows you to sell more or increase margins?

■ Think about how advantages can be combined to produce a virtuous competitive cycle. Can you do something short term that can increase margins? Can you use those margins to invest in further differentiation?

■ Take the time to look creatively at how lessons from other industries can apply to yours. How could you radically change business models? How can you reverse assumptions in a way that would give you sustainable competitive advantage?

Related ideas

Jim Collins, in his book *Good to Great*, argues that small improvements can eventually create a kind of flywheel effect. Each provides momentum for the next until the overall advantage is sufficient to really surpass the competition. You don't have to start big. You can work on little advantages, understand them and then combine them gradually. These become your core competencies, they work together in the kind of value chain described on page 175 and – because you have taken so long to develop them – are hard to imitate.

Making strategic decisions and choices

Your company is a collection of decisions. You have to choose your market. You need to decide on your products. Every part of the business is the result of actions, and all those actions have decisions attached to them. Strategy is about decisions.

Frequency: Depends on the decisions.
Key participants: Leadership first.
Strategy rating: **

Coca-Cola today is the result of every decision it has ever made. In the nineteenth century, its founder decided to develop a non-alcoholic drink in response to US prohibition. He claimed it was a medicine that cured many diseases. In 1887, he decided to sell his company to a group including Asa Griggs Candler, who turned out to be a marketing genius. Candler made the decision to run a design competition for the, now iconic, coke contour bottle.

Thirty years ago, the management decided to launch a new coke, which was unpopular. Within three months they decided to go back to the original formula. Later, they decided to diversify into healthy drinks including investing in smoothie maker, Innocent.

In 2014, the CEO made another multi-billion dollar decision to invest into fast-growing energy drinks maker, Monster, and joined forces with coffee machine maker Keurig to develop a cold-brew machine to deliver Coke-in-a-Pod. In 2015, the company expressed concern about FIFA corruption allegations, but decided to stay as a World Cup sponsor. Coca-Cola tomorrow is about decisions made today and yesterday.

Objective

Strategy is a stream of decisions and actions. Some decisions are very informal. Some are very formal. Some decisions end badly. Some decisions end well. Some decisions open up possibilities while other decisions close down opportunities. As a strategist you either influence decisions, or make them.

It's good to be aware of how decisions can be influenced. There are various forces that limit your range of decisions. Some people argue that strategy is the art of the possible: you can only really choose between options that are already possible in the world as it is. But strategy can also use what is possible now to do things in the future that are impossible now.

Context

Every company starts with a decision (like the Coca-Cola example), and the whole history of the company is made up of big and little decisions with big and little consequences. You will only find out whether a decision was smart or helpful *after* you've made the decision.

Strategy decisions are meant to be about the big picture (see page 51) but some big decisions turn out to have a small impact. And often there are small decisions that have a big (or strategic) impact. There are also decisions that appear to be urgent and those that seem less urgent.

It can be useful to examine decisions to see what kind of priority can be given to them. But it's important to remember that their importance can change and that different kinds of decisions matter to strategy in different ways. It's worth asking whether a decision is strategic because it will:

- get specific things done;
- outmanoeuvre the competition;
- be part of a strategic pattern;
- fix the company's position;
- risk (or save) the company's future.

This last point matters. If it's going to risk or save the company's future then you want to get it right. It's the most important decision – so it's the most strategic decision. If you have the resources to cope with the decision being wrong then you can make the decision more comfortably. If you don't then you really are taking a wild (but perhaps necessary) gamble (see page 209).

Challenge

It's impossible to make the perfect decision, but it's worth trying to make smarter decisions. The challenge is to make sure you keep making decisions that are fast enough to get the right things done.

Decision making is not completely rational or objective. You can never have all the information you need and your decisions will always be based on subjective considerations – and a lot of those will be invisible even to you.

You might gather facts that only support your argument (and ignore anything that threatens your position). Decisions can be inconsistent because you can't quite figure out how you made the decision last time. You may see patterns that don't really exist or think that there is a link between cause and effect that just isn't true. Your optimism or pessimism will also affect your decisions.

- Have you considered the other side of your argument?
- Are you making decisions based on what you have always done?
- What assumptions are you using? Have you tested them?
- Are failings based on good/bad luck? Or good/bad decisions?
- What part does optimism or pessimism play in your decision?
- Are your decisions based on an accurate view of the long and short term?

Another challenge is to make decisions fast enough to be worthwhile. An imperfect decision may be enough to get activity started, which is better than doing nothing. Or no decision may be better than wasting time and resources.

- What will happen if you make no decision?
- What will happen if you make the wrong decision?

- Will the decision create more opportunities?
- Will the decision limit future opportunities?

The good news is that thinking about how you make decisions will help make better decisions. It will improve your ability to cope flexibly with the consequences of those decisions. And it will involve people in the assumptions built into decisions so that they can adapt when they change.

Success

As a leader, you need to make strategic decisions. It's one of your main roles. If you don't make decisions then there are consequences. People may not know what to do – there is confusion over which direction to take. People may not do anything because they are waiting for a decision. Or they may all do different things, leading to waste and ineffective action.

You'll know you're getting better at strategic decision making when you have a clearer idea of when a decision is strategic. You will see opportunities and threats in the consequences of making a decision. You will have a priority system – in your head or on paper – that helps you organise decisions.

You will also be aware of potential bias. Think about why a decision has been made. Try to see different points of view. Subject them to tough criticism. Reverse your assumptions. Consider whether decisions are leading to strategic decline. If you keep making similar patterns of decisions, will the company die?

Strategists' measures of success

- You are aware of different kinds of bias.
- Decisions are made in a framework that prioritises their urgency and impact.
- Assumptions are open, so that people can support or challenge.
- Flexibility is built into the way you cope with the consequences of decisions.
- Your decisions open up possibilities, leading to new opportunities.

Pitfalls

Thinking about decisions can slow the company down. People can start to over-think what they are deciding. They can worry about consequences or start to waste time applying models and frameworks. Involving bigger groups in decisions can be good for engagement. It can be helpful for generating ideas but should not be allowed to degenerate into no decision being made. The aim is not to stop decisions but to make your decisions smarter.

Strategists' checklist

- Use one of the decision-making tools (see page 163) to look at different aspects of decisions.

- Explore decisions that are made. How urgent are they? How important are they? Which decisions have been delayed for years? Why?

- How can you increase your knowledge about making a decision? Some decisions are easy with experience.

- Question patterns of decisions that are very similar. Are they leading the company somewhere dangerous? Is everyone thinking the same way just out of habit? What happens if you reverse the logic of decisions?

- Be aware that decisions have a habitual, political and chaotic aspect to them. Decisions get made for many emotional reasons. And decisions get ignored for many emotional reasons.

Related ideas

David Hickson's research concluded that how long a strategic decision takes to make and how long a strategic decisions takes to be put into action does not automatically determine success.

Some, like Constantinos Markides, argue that being second can be better than being first. Waiting gives you a chance to get the decision right, so you can learn from the decisions of others.

Other research, like that led by Fernando Suarez of Boston University School of Management, suggests that there is a 'window of opportunity' for certain kinds of strategic decisions. You can win big by not being too early or too late.

The most important thing is to think strategically and flexibly about how decisions are made so that even when the wrong decision is made, your actions make it right (see page 148 and 154).

Making the best of any particular situation is similar to the ideas described at the end of the last chapter. Causal thinking seeks resources to achieve goals. Effectual thinking seeks goals that can be achieved with available resources.

Smart strategists move between effectual and causal decisions. They ask questions about what they need to get to where they want. And where they can get to with what they have. They can often achieve more than tactical entrepreneurs because they see further, and more than long range planners because they see differently.

What actually happens, as Marc de Rond, professor at Cambridge University, points out, is a mix of choice, chance events, and initial conditions: some advantageous, others problematic, threatening or even traumatic.

It is here that ideas from psychology about resilience and post-traumatic growth, associated with Lawrence Calhoun and Richard Tedeschi, are helpful. Resilience responds to failures, including wrong decisions, with persistence. Post-traumatic growth is about a struggle with purpose that leads to better places and performance.

Adapting to your competitive environment

Your strategy will depend – in part – on how well it fits the competitive situation. Stable markets where competition is low may require a different approach to chaotic markets where competition is high. The approach to the situation is not fixed but it must fit.

Frequency: Continually.
Key participants: Everyone.
Strategy rating: **

In 2002, Walmart became the world's largest company based on revenue. By 2014, it had revenues of $485 million ($40 billion more than Shell in second place). It has over 11,000 stores worldwide.

Walmart became the world's largest company by following a formula of great everyday value supported by an efficient supply chain. Rules for success were centrally enforced to ensure rapid expansion. Walmart was better adapted to a primarily American competitive environment where the moves of competitors and tastes of customers were well known.

The growth of Walmart also led to new challenges. It is facing aggressive new competitors in its home markets. Under pressure to grow it has moved into unfamiliar markets – like urban centres – where its rules of success don't necessarily work. It has also had to deal with upmarket moves from competitors – like Target – and small format rivals – like Aldi (see page 62). To grow, it has become more flexible with some autonomy granted to change the central model.

Objective

To try to adapt to the demands of a market, it is useful to describe the competitive environment you are facing. The 5 forces model (see page 169) helps by identifying the activities of existing competitors, new entrants, suppliers, substitute products and services, and customers. Other models included in the toolkit help to define various aspects of the market.

- What level of competition are you facing?
- Is the level of competition increasing or decreasing?
- Are the actions of competitors becoming more or less certain?

The next step is to consider what kind of organisation you have, and whether it is a good fit for the competitive challenge you face. The working assumption is that highly competitive environments need highly adaptable organisations. The assumption is that you want your structure to involve people, your leadership style to be more informal and your culture to be open to change – indeed welcoming of it. But it's not quite that simple.

Context

One approach to dealing with uncertainty and high levels of competition is to take steps to create a more organic organisation.

There is a standard organic recipe. Decentralisation moves decisions away from the head office to the field (or even to the front line). An attempt is made to increase informality. The relevant people are able to contribute based on their knowledge (and interest) rather than their position in the hierarchy.

Following this approach, the response to dealing with certainty and lower levels of competition is to create a more mechanistic organisation.

There is also a standard mechanistic recipe. Centralisation drags decisions back from the front line to the head office (or even all the way back to the CEO). An attempt is made to increase formality. Hierarchy, forms, standards and processes are implemented that seek to control contributions and actions.

Both of these are useful starting points to understanding possible responses to differing levels of competition and uncertainty.

- What kind of organisation are you working with?
- What kind of competitive environment are you facing?

- Is there a good fit?
- Are there obvious conflicts?
- What could be done to create a better fit?

In reality, there is no simple fit between one type of environment and one type of organisation. There are more criteria to consider for both environment and organisation and the combination leading to success is not straightforward.

Challenge

One challenge is that standard recipes rarely lead to competitive advantage. If everyone seeks to follow the same recipe then they usually just reduce differentiation and – unwittingly – increase direct competition.

In practice, it's also impossible for everyone to follow the same recipe identically so you will automatically have varying levels of organic and mechanistic. The key is to understand these differences as opportunities.

Ideally, you want to know more about your environment than simply its levels of competitiveness and uncertainty. You want to know the way your market environment works: its particular shape, rhythm and peculiarities. So, ask yourself:

- Independent of the market, how well has the company been doing? Is your performance increasing or decreasing? Has it been constant or variable? Your choices can have an impact on success beyond the general trends of your market (see page 56).
- What market conditions are beyond your control? If no one wants your particular kind of product then you'll have to start making something else or figure out how to change the market. If there is a global recession you have to find ways of thriving but you can't single-handedly reverse the recession.
- What explains the performance of the company? You can compare your company in a few ways to its rivals. What are your costs? What do customers want? What are competitors doing? How is the industry doing? What are your strengths and weaknesses? (see page 167)

Cost analysis gives you a better idea of how costs work within your company (and industry). It involves some specific microeconomic techniques to answer some valuable questions. In comparison to your competitors:

- Are your costs lower or higher?
- Are your prices lower or higher?
- Are your returns on investment higher or lower?
- Are there better things you could be doing with your money?
- Are there certain fixed costs that stop you changing prices or profits?
- How do your variable costs compare?
- What can be changed about your cost structure in the short term and long term?
- At what point do you reach diminishing returns if you invest more?
- How much more can be invested to benefit from greater efficiencies of economies of scale and economies of scope?

Demand analysis gives you a better idea of customer behaviour related to price and value. It also involves microeconomic techniques to answer valuable questions:

- Does demand rise or fall when you increase or decrease prices?
- What can be done to change demand elasticity in your favour?

Usually the higher the price the lower the number of paying customers, but that's not the whole story. Different products have different elasticity of demand. Alcohol and fuel prices have to change a lot before there is any difference in demand – on an industry level – because there are few alternatives.

But on a company basis, if there is no difference between what you offer and what competitors offer then the price really does matter. That's why it can be so valuable to follow a differentiation strategy – so that you can keep prices higher without losing overall revenue (see page 189 as an example).

A situation where there is only one price possible for a product is unusual. This perfect competition requires perfect information and identical products, including the location they are available and the way they are sold. But with increasing online competition and transparency of information, it is now harder for companies to charge multiple prices for the same product.

Market analysis gives you a better understanding of the shape of competition that you have to face. It asks valuable questions:

- How many companies compete in the market?
- What is the structure of the market?
- How different are products and services?

You might be facing perfect competition with many companies and no chance of differentiation. But it's more likely you are facing imperfect competition because although there are many companies you have found ways of being different. You could be dealing with an oligopoly where there are a few competitors with no differentiation. You could also be in a dominant position where because of differentiation you have reduced your effective competitors.

Success

You've made progress when you understand the nature of your market and competitive environment. You want to know the level of competition, the number of competitors, the level of stability and the possibilities for innovation.

You'll also understand more about the demand characteristics for your kind of product. You want to know what is likely to happen if you raise or drop prices. You also want to know what you could do to change the cost characteristics of your company so that you can change prices without damaging your profit margins. You may even reach a point of cost leadership (see page 171) which allows you to use many strategic games (see page 83).

You will also remember that all of this analysis is about figuring out more effective ways of achieving your overall strategic intentions. Or even of discovering strategic intentions that will deliver your overall objectives. Your aim is to find ways of differentiating your product or placing your company in a position to succeed despite a lack of differentiation. Both options are open.

You will also think carefully about how well your organisation fits with the demands of its competitive environment and strategic intention. Are you slow where you should be quick? Are you chaotic when you should be stable?

Strategists' measures of success

→ Your team has a basic grasp of the competitive dynamics you face.

→ Your company understands the different organisational options and choices.

→ Analysis of demand, market and costs gives you more options for strategy.

→ You are actively looking for ways to create strategy and business models that can differentiate sufficiently for growth.

Pitfalls

It's entirely possible to succeed without detailed analysis. And it's possible for analysis paralysis to occur so that your detailed knowledge takes the place of effective action. Strategy is about shaping the future much more than it is about just understanding economic models and techniques. So be careful not to become lost in economic models – or to become difficult to understand because you speak in the language of economic models.

Strategists' checklist

▨ Discuss your organisational style, leadership approach, structure and culture. Think about how they are appropriate or inappropriate, helpful or unhelpful to your strategic challenges. There are no perfect versions of mechanistic or organic. There is only what works or does not work.

▨ Explore what microeconomic concepts and techniques can offer. Be careful not to get lost in the detail of analysis. Often deep experience with a business can give people an understanding of cost and demand dynamics. Use both analysis and experience to challenge assumptions but try not to make obvious mistakes because of lack of knowledge.

■ Don't accept the given wisdom of a market too easily. There are always ways of growing a market by changing some aspect of your business or business model. Your product can be sold to another market or customer. You can sell it in a different way. You can even use your existing organisational resources and capabilities to do something completely different.

■ Think about what would happen if a competitor or new entrant changed the market dynamic your company has been used to. How would you adapt? Would you survive? What would help or hurt you? (See page 56.)

■ Use the strategy toolkit and principles throughout this book to find niches, competitive approaches and unique combinations of product, price, positioning and plots to change the accepted rules in your favour. Everything from advertising, to efficiency, to design, to customer experience can help you adapt successfully to the demands of the market.

Related ideas

Tom Burns and George Stalker originated the terms 'mechanistic' and 'organic'. Their book – *The Management of Innovation* – argues for a contingency view of strategy. They suggest moving to a more organic organisation as levels of uncertainty increase.

Martin Reeves and Knut Haanaes argue something similar in *Your Strategy Needs a Strategy*. They identify four strategic styles depending on the malleability and uncertainty of your environment; 'classical', finding a niche through investment; 'adaptive', organising for fast reactions to changing tastes; 'shaping', changing the ecosystem in your favour; and 'visionary', longer term version of shaping that changes the nature of competition to capture future opportunities.

four

Winning with strategy

Strategy is about getting to where you'd like to be, or at least making the most of where you are. And this is part of what it means to win with strategy. You don't have to win at all costs and you don't have to play a zero sum game where there is only one winner and a whole bunch of sorry losers.

Winning with strategy can mean competing directly. It can mean using the resources and tools available to get ahead of someone else. For some people it means doing whatever it takes to destroy the competition. But that's about the ethics of the people using the tools of strategy. You don't have to be destructive or vindictive. You could use strategy to win by creating value.

Strategists can choose to create new markets rather than just getting to the top of the one they are in. The ethical strategist can deliberately limit certain options because they are unethical. The caring strategist can find ways of winning that help communities and those who have the least amount of power. The creative strategist can bring artists and engineers together to produce beauty that enhances the lives of other people.

Strategy doesn't belong only to MBAs and management consultants. It is a collection of different ways of understanding the present to shape the future. So you can find out what you do best and try to find room for that in a busy world that may not realise what you are offering.

There are lots of great ideas that never become real because the people who have those ideas don't know how to get support for them. Understanding the language of strategy can help to get the funding and resources that you need.

Look at the strategist's toolkit. You can explore how the different parts of an organisation fit together into a value chain. Some people don't like the words, but the model works because it's a powerful simplification of the real world. What each person and department does can increase or decrease the overall value of what you offer to people.

And beyond your offices, the way you fit into the work of other people also matters. You can learn about how to connect the best of what you do (core competencies) with the best of what other people do. And you can consider how to grow your organisation so that it can make a contribution. If you want to change the world, strategy is still the shortest route from means to ends.

Winning strategy games

Sometimes strategy is about competing. It isn't the only way to play the game but it's a choice that is available to you. You may want to choose from a variety of classic strategies to win decisively. It is even more valuable to create a virtuous cycle of growth and advantage.

Frequency: Consider different games regularly.
Key participants: You and your team.
Strategy rating: ****

The founders of Zara, who became one of the world's richest married couples, believe in staying very close to what customers want. And by what the customer wants, they mean what customers buy and wear. Traditionally, high street fashion gamble on two annual collections. Each gamble taken more than a year ahead. Each outsourced to the cheapest possible manufacturer, often thousands of miles away. Zara doesn't like guessing or waiting.

To win at this fast-fashion game, Zara made its own rules. New products replace old products twice a week. Customers find this compelling. Zara looks carefully, and quickly, at what is hot and what is not. They drop what doesn't sell, and replace it with variations of what is popular. They send people to fashion shows to send back photos for inspiration. These are compared with a huge database of previous products, to speed up design and manufacture. The results attract fashionistas on a budget, but also royalty and movie stars.

Around eighty per cent of their clothes are made locally, to keep the design-to-sale cycle under 30 days. Only particularly complex pieces are made further away, and Zara has rigorous standards for employees in all factories. Their stores aim to create a multi-mirrored wardrobe experience, where customers can create their own looks without noise or interruption. They want customers to get what they want, to keep them coming back for more. This is how Zara wins.

Objective

It is easy enough to talk about competitive advantage but it is often difficult for businesses to get beyond such simple concepts as having the lowest costs or having a unique product feature.

After you've done the hard work necessary to have a competitive advantage, it can be even harder to maintain your advantage. Someone else can reduce the price – by improving productivity, finding cheaper employees or just by accepting lower margins. Or a competitor simply copies your unique product feature.

- How can you turn temporary advantages into decisive advantages?
- What can you do to create space between you and your competitors?
- How can a virtuous cycle of growth and advantage be established?

Thinking like a strategist (see Part one) is essential to seeing how to connect a stream of actions in ways that competitors don't understand and cannot match. Each successful action leaves you in a better place to take the next action. You gather more resources and more possibilities with which you can construct even greater improvements and further difficult-to-copy benefits.

This isn't about breaking laws or being unethical. It isn't about being greedy either. It's about connecting the dots. It's about moving from basic advantages and value offered to the customer to deep advantages and value. This is good for customers and can only be achieved by creating decisive advantage.

Context

While the exact combination of strategies you use will have to be unique, there are components, example strategies you can work with. There is less written about them than other aspects of strategy, which emphasises their value to you as a strategist.

Overwhelming competitors with focused energy can create the space you need. If your company is unleashed in an organised and focused way it will come as such a surprise to your competitors that they are unable to respond.

Exploit exceptions that your competitors don't understand or are not motivated to look after. Looking after non-customers is one approach to finding exceptions (see page 215). Going into the field and looking for insights, problems and contradictions is another (see pages 217 and 193).

Threatening the profit of competitors is a way of distracting them and weakening their cash position but can also leave you in a negative game where you each progressively lose money. It's one way of encouraging a competitor to retreat, leaving you to enjoy less competition, but there are other more positive approaches.

Creating your own version is all about improving on existing ideas. You might start with a basic copy but pretty soon you imaginatively move your idea beyond the original concept. Target did it to Walmart who did it to K-Mart. Apple did it to Microsoft with their iPad Tablet. Uber are doing it to every taxi company with a customer experience deficit.

Breaking compromises is part of exploiting exceptions and creating your own version. If you can find a rule that everyone keeps, and then successfully break that rule to the benefit of your customers, you have the start of a decisive advantage. Four Seasons hotels used free toiletries for guests as the basis for enduring success. First, because no other hotel offered the same benefits, and second, because they gained a reputation for great customer service. More recently, Airbnb have broken the rules to turn homes into (unique) hotels where everyone 'belongs everywhere'.

Challenge

Each of the hardball strategies above – and others like them – is difficult. To overwhelm a competitor requires a level of organisation that is hard to achieve. And you have to take a risk that this is the right time and the right gamble.

Similarly, threatening the profit of competitors can be very costly. The ideal is to use it defensively to keep them away from your areas of profit. Or to only threaten profit in market segments they are happy to leave because they appear unattractive to them. This creates a dilemma for your competitor, who knows you want the market but doesn't want to compete.

Exploiting exceptions, creating your own version and breaking compromises all rely on the ability to have fairly unique insights. These insights come from a combination of creativity and expertise that require investment of time and money. Your first efforts may be less hard to copy than you had imagined or less valuable in creating demand than you had hoped.

Use the strategist's toolkit as part of team activities to play out scenarios in which you move from where you are now through successive phases of competitive advantage. Each time imagine how advantages at one stage can open up possibilities for the next stage.

Success

You'll know that you're getting better when you are confident at speaking about different kinds of strategic games. You will learn to use the strategist's toolkit to identify opportunities that your competitors will find hard to exploit.

You will recognise the dangers of such hardball strategies to your own company. And you will think about your response to them. How will you deal with threats to your profits? How can you re-act effectively to attempts to overwhelm you? Who are the most likely competitors to play those games? What areas are you being led away from because they appear unattractive?

Your team will start to view strategy as a mixture of thinking, planning and *playing*. There are games to be played that make the best of your thinking and planning, without which they are wasted.

Strategists' measures of success

→ Individual games are understood in relation to general strategy.

→ Teams use the games to play scenarios through as part of planning.

→ You do not rely on negative games and instead use your knowledge to be ready for attacks from competitors.

→ Cumulative, decisive competitive advantage is created.

Pitfalls

Some strategies are played just to damage competitors. They become so negative that whole markets become locked in a negative spiral of reducing returns. If you rely too heavily on negative strategies your company may spend too little time on improving your own offer through innovation. You may also damage your brand reputation and risk attracting the attention of government.

Strategists' checklist

■ Explore how competitive advantages could be developed into a stream of advantages that reinforce your competitive position.

■ Consider actions that put your competitors at a disadvantage and give you time and resources to invest in improving your products and services, or to invest in talent or resources.

■ Start to think about strategy as a series of connected actions rather than as stand-alone plans.

■ Draw up a strategic campaign with your team to increase focus and commitment on the creativity necessary to establish a longer-term advantage (and contribution).

■ Be careful not to depend on negative competitive strategies. Their purpose should be to protect positive strategies.

■ Consider your response to competitors who use this kind of strategy against you. Being aware can avoid competitive traps and dead ends.

Related ideas

George Stalk and Rob Lachenauer argue – in their book *Hardball* – that competitive advantage is no longer enough because it is so short-lived. The more important focus is to transform momentary advantage into perpetual advantage. This moves from a kind of blue ocean strategy (see page 189) into a resource-based advantage over time (see page 177).

Perpetual advantage combines what you do and where you do it. In their latest book, *Playing to Win*, A.G. Lafley and Roger Martin urge strategists to ask: What's your winning aspiration? Where will you play? How will you win? What capabilities must you have? And what management systems are required?

Creating new markets

You don't have to compete in exactly the same market as your competitors. With imagination and effort you can create new markets that have less competition. You can take existing products and focus on non-traditional customers. Or you can create new products for existing customers, or you can create new products for new customers.

Frequency: Examine carefully at least annually.
Key participants: Your team.
Strategy rating: ***

Zipcar offers you the benefits of car ownership without the inconveniences. It isn't car rental in the traditional sense because you pay to use the car by the hour. It isn't car ownership because you don't have to tax, insure and maintain it. For a simple monthly fee, you can find and access a shiny new vehicle via smartphone or smartwatch, before parking it safely for the next member. Avis bought them for $500 million to have access to this new market. Fifteen years after launch, ZipCar had nearly one million members – and new competitors, large and small, trying hard to take a slice.

Objective

Competing on price is dangerous. Even if you succeed in being the lowest-cost provider, you will probably have reduced the total size and margins in your market. It's more attractive (although diffi-cult) to compete on creating new markets. This can be done by fo-cusing on a particular niche with existing products *or* by making your product so different that it creates a new market.

Context

It is possible for identical products to create large profits. There are certain commodities (oil, for instance) where the raw material is limited in supply and valuable even in its unprocessed form.

But after the raw material stage it becomes harder to create high margins if products and services are identical.

Indeed, it is in no one's interest if every company is supplying an identical service or product to every customer. The organisations have to compete on price, leading to lower overall returns. The customer has to accept products and services that are made for everyone rather than something that has been designed with more specific requirements.

If there are advantages gained through experience then the first to market has potential benefits. If there are advantages gained through size then growing aggressively has potential benefits. If experience and size are combined with benefits of specialisation then there will be a strong trend towards a monopoly.

- How can we do specialise to create a new market?
- How can we benefit from our experience to protect our market?
- How can we benefit from our size to protect our new market?

You may not want a situation with no competition. Other competitors can help you create the market. Their effort added to your effort can educate potential customers about the benefits of your product and service. You can learn from their ideas and their mistakes. They may attract suppliers that you need to support the overall ideas.

Yet as part of creating you need to be looking around you at your competitors in your strategic groups. The important part is to understand their assumptions and how they are likely to move or not move in response to any strategic moves you make. It makes sense to select moves that are original enough to discourage competitors from immediately copying them.

You may want to launch the new product or service without significant publicity to slow down a response from your traditional competitors. Reach out to existing customers, or via existing customers to new kinds of customers. You also need to look at how companies you don't normally deal with will respond. There is only so much consumer money to go around at any one time so you may be taking money from others who respond aggressively.

Dominant companies will spend huge amounts of money to stop new innovators getting comfortable in their new markets. When P&G introduced a new bleach product – Vibrant – into a test market, the immediate rival – Clorox – bought a gallon of bleach for every household in the area. When Netscape introduced a new browser, the immediate rival – Microsoft – gave away its competing product for free to everyone in the world. Google did something similar with its low-cost Android operating system, eventually forcing Microsoft to provide upgrades free of charge to Windows 10.

The reason for thinking about competitors isn't to stop you creating a new market. It is to create strategies that anticipate their actions. If the product is being offered at a price point that is not attractive to the dominant players then they are less likely to do anything about you. If you offer something that is truly innovative, price is less of an issue and it will take longer for them to respond.

A particularly good way is to simplify an existing product so that the competitor is confused because they can't see why fewer features are more attractive than their existing product. This kind of strategic thinking is what allows an innovative product to thrive beyond the usual competitive games from the status quo.

Challenge

You're looking for a way of creating new markets or new space in an existing market. You are seeking to innovate in some way that produces greater demand for the type of product or service. Or you want to find a new type of product or service to sell to existing customers.

In simple terms, this may come from either some huge differentiating advantage or a collection of relatively small advantages.

If you are the first with a product that is significantly better for a particular customer group and those advantages can be protected by law (or secrecy) then your advantage may be huge. The trouble is that finding and protecting such an advantage is very difficult. And any protection you have may be only temporary as legal and technological challenges are made to your position.

Pharmaceutical companies have traditionally depended on this kind of (blockbuster) competitive advantage but it has become more difficult. Technology companies also use patent protection, and sue and counter-sue to try to get some defence against competitors. Apple, Microsoft, Facebook, Amazon and Samsung all regularly play the legal game.

Some of this legal activity buys them time. Apple protected certain features of its original iPod including the click wheel. Without the protection, it would have been copied more easily by competitors who might have succeeded in hiding some of the other advantages of the iPod. The same has been true of the one-click buying process with Amazon or the news feed on Facebook.

Despite this, most competitive advantage is something that other companies can't copy for a variety of reasons. Or something they haven't copied yet because they haven't had enough time. You get to create a new market or niche if you can collect together a number of advantages that position you distinctly from other companies.

Success

The first step is to find a competitive advantage that will create a new market (segment or niche). You might want to go after non-customers who are not understood by existing suppliers.

- Why don't existing products appeal to non-customers?
- How could new products and services be designed that would be more popular?
- How could the assumptions of existing products be reversed or modified to be valuable to non-customers?

You could also look at existing customers in new ways:

- How could you serve existing customers better?
- How could you serve existing customers differently?

Consider the example of Levi's, who sell denim clothing. They tried to protect their clothing from being sold in supermarkets because they wanted to maintain the big competitive advantage of advertising-led brand value.

They have now decided to focus their creative efforts on serving customers in new ways to create new markets. For instance, they invested in research to find new cuts of jeans that would fit different body shapes. This curve ID brand delivers a competitive advantage because each customer finds a better fit.

They have also started working with specialists in different lifestyle groups to gain insights into how to create denim wear suitable for different activities. For example, they have worked on jeans and jackets designed specifically for cyclists. This focus and attention to detail creates multiple advantages and new markets of which their competitors are not even aware.

The basis of their competitive advantage is only slightly removed from their core abilities. They know how to mass produce, distribute and retail denim products. This effort extends their core skills *and* their core markets by focusing on the distinct needs of particular non-core customer groups.

At first, think about how to create growth by offering products to groups at price points below and above your core customers. The value customer and the luxury customer (relative to your existing position) are worth exploring.

This is why VW, for example, offer customers SKODA and SEAT at the price-conscious end all the way up to Lamborghini and Bentley for the wealthy image-obsessive. But it's a particular combination of price, performance, customer experience, design, advertising and heritage that allows them to look after and create new markets.

Strategists' measures of success

- You have found out why non-customers don't buy existing products.
- You have designed new ways of delivering value to non-customers.
- You have uncovered ways in which existing customers are being underserved.
- You have created new ways of offering specialist products and services.
- You can combine focus and differentiation to create new markets and niches.

Pitfalls

It's possible to confuse new markets with new features. In this case, you just keep on adding new features that are aimed at new customer groups without actually creating new value. This can increase the cost of delivering products and services while actually reducing the value they see in them.

Building your new features around stereotypical understanding of customer segments is dangerous. It's also a mistake to underestimate the new skills and resources needed to deliver new features. If you try to deliver to a group you don't understand, the chances are that you will create new ways of losing money rather than new markets.

Strategists' checklist

- Plot your existing core market in terms of price and performance.

- Think about how to create new markets by offering modified products and services to the luxury and basic customers.

- Consider how your product can be used by non-customers – those who may have the same amount of money as your core customers but don't use your product. It isn't about price or performance but some other reason. Find out why and you have the beginnings of a new market.

- Play about with your product. Make an extreme version. Something many times smaller or faster or bigger. Change the colour, the material, and underline different aspects of its design. You may find that a secondary market can be created that will one day be bigger than your original market.

- Observe customers using your products and services. Try to find examples where customers are adapting your product for uses that you never intended originally. Lubricant manufacturers

WD-40 ask customers to come forward with new ways of using the product, which they can advertise – without changing the product in any material way.

▇ Look for trade-offs between prices, performance and features. Find new ways of overcoming those trade-offs (so you can offer higher performance at lower prices) or where you can offer superior performance for which a much higher price can be achieved.

▇ Stay flexible with the bases of competition. You might assume they are the traditional differentiators, but then you will always be stuck competing in the same old ways. Bring in creative ideas from outside of your industry and innovate at all points inside and outside the product.

Related ideas

Creating new markets can use ideas from economics about the concept of value. The idea is to increase value that the customer receives more than the price he pays compared to any competitor so that he will buy his product from you and not your competitor. The task of strategy is to find a way of maximising your margins and the customer's value.

It is worth remembering that value is not fixed. Instead, its an ever-changing pattern of decisions and opinions. The terms 'value network' and 'value constellation' have been used to illustrate the way that various producers and consumers interact.

Some evidence suggests that it is best to let the market pull you towards what customers think is valuable. Other research concludes that valuable resources can be developed and then be pushed towards customers who will recognise value they didn't know they wanted.

Getting ahead of your strategic group

With a clever strategy, each action is self-reinforcing. Each action creates more options and advantages that are mutually beneficial. Each victory is not just for today but for tomorrow. Consider the strategic trajectory of your plan and how each part may provide the basis for future success. This is the test of creative, forward-thinking strategy.

Frequency: Quarterly.
Key participants: You and your boss.
Strategy rating: ****

Amazon started as an online book shop. Its key competitors were traditional real-world book shops because that is where traditional customers bought their traditional books. But it also had other online competitors which it has surpassed. Amazon chose to focus on service – knowing and serving customers better than any other book store.

This ability to deliver superior service has allowed them to judge what to do by asking whether it helped the customer. The service foundation allowed them to move into new markets and services – like Kindle, the eBook reader, and Prime, a subscription bundle that includes free delivery and streaming video. This service strategy informed its acquisitions of like-minded companies – like audible.com and zappos.com – and allowed Amazon to see the opportunities in delivering the Cloud as a business service. No other retailer has managed such rapid growth or relentless innovation.

Objective

Moving past your competitors is part of corporate strategy. You look around the competitors who share most similarities with you. These similarities will be a mixture of characteristics.

Some competitors will share location – those closest to you or those competing in the same geographical markets. Some will share size or revenue characteristics. Others will sell similar products, services or look after the same or similar customers. They are your strategic group.

You don't have to compete directly with companies in your strategic group. But they may be trying to compete directly with you. Even if you decide not to compete directly you may find them a useful place to begin your differentiation efforts.

- How is market share divided in your strategic group?
- What are the traditional differentiating characteristics in your strategic group? Is it about relative quality and price, or something else?
- How does profitability and revenue vary across the strategic group?
- Who is growing fastest? Who has been around the longest?
- What are the strengths and weaknesses of each group member?
- Where is the innovation coming from?
- What is the basis of competitive advantage?

At the simplest level, find out whether competition between members of the strategic group is about price, focus or differentiation (see pages 169 and 171) and then look deeper at the sources of those advantages. What is each company known for? What are they selling?

Understanding the group gives you a sense of your own possibilities. If they can do it then you can try to copy them, exceed them, or offer something different. You may find considerable variance among your competition as well as remarkable similarities. Knowing more can better shape your own competitive actions and strategy.

Also look around the edges of your strategic group. Examine replacement (or substitute) products and new entrants for threats that could change the status quo. Does the existing situation help you? If you are weak in your strategic group, it may make sense to consider ways of disrupting the status quo. If you are strong, it may be the ideal time to consider ways of further strengthening your position or trying to disrupt things before a smaller rival gets there first.

Context

You do not need to be limited by your strategic group, but it can be very helpful to understand it. Most businesses are started in response to strategic groups. Either a person learns the rules of the strategic group and copies them or they react to a perceived gap or weakness by starting a business to do something different.

One approach to seeing a strategic group more clearly is to map out its members related to a couple of competitive characteristics. These strategic maps help to clarify the positioning of the members of a group.

Strategic maps can also help you to consider where the strategic space is most crowded and where the opportunities exist. For example, if every retailer is serving the high-fashion, mid-price market then the opportunity is to look after top (luxury) or bottom (value) segments.

Strategic maps along the traditional dimensions of competition can also be creatively extended into multiple dimensions. Consider what differentiates your strategic competitors in addition to their positioning on the strategic map.

- Why are they doing better or worse than you are?
- How do they try to differentiate themselves?
- Do they move faster? Are they aiming at a younger or older customer?
- Is their brand more distinctive? More radical?
- Are they doing anything distinctive in advertising or marketing?
- Do they have a different value or supply chain?

The objective is to understand other companies well enough to know how to respond, copy, improve or differentiate. You are not locked into the limitations of your strategic group. However, it makes no sense to completely ignore their existence since you may provoke them into direct competition whether you want it or not.

Laker Airways was the first no-frills budget airline operating trans-atlantic flights. The company looked at its strategic group and found that all had ignored the budget traveller because their high costs and complexity made it unprofitable. Laker started very successfully with a number of innovations but had ignored the ability of its strategic group to start a price war that it could not win. As a result, it went bankrupt within five years of starting.

Virgin Airlines learned from the strategic mistakes of Laker. It understood something of the hardball tactics and 'dirty tricks' campaigns that might be expected from traditional rivals. It also learned that it needed to have a range of services that would allow it to compete throughout the year and which did not depend mainly on price.

Ryanair, easyJet, Southwest and jetBlue were all examples of budget airlines who learned to avoid some of the direct competition. They set out differences more clearly and backed those up by strategic ways of operating that made it hard for traditional rivals to compete.

This kind of learning about the dynamics of strategic groups helps to increase the chances that your innovations (or your blocking tactics) will be successful. Ignorance may be a useful way of questioning accepted norms and finding new strategies and business models. But experience is still hugely helpful in avoiding obvious rookie mistakes or adopting a fatally flawed strategic plan.

Challenge

Looking across the history of your strategic sector also helps you with the challenge of knowing how change tends to have an impact. You – as a strategic thinker – are developing a view of the bigger picture (see page 51).

- How often do changes happen in your industry?
- How have members of your strategic group reacted in the past?
- What is the kind of change that they fear? What do they understand?

First you want to find the basis of competition in your existing strategic space faced with the actions of your immediate strategic group. You want to know how to play the traditional rules to avoid being squeezed on – for example: price, market share, profitability or brand value. You want to recognise signs that someone is coming after you and have a range of scenarios in mind for responding (see page 183).

The next step is to identify new strategic spaces into which you could move. These may be existing markets that are new to you so you want to understand enough to anticipate the significant strategic responses of your new strategic group. These may include new markets that you want to create (see page 91). Even here it is possible to anticipate who you are threatening and how customers and competitors will respond.

Another benefit of identifying new (or nearby) strategic spaces is that it prepares you for where competition might come from. If you're thinking of disrupting someone else's space then they may be thinking of doing the same.

- Is it easier/harder to move to luxury?
- Is it easier/harder to move to bargain?
- Can you blur the boundaries of what they offer and what you already offer? Can you turn products into services or services into products?
- Can you change the nature of the business model that is offered?
- Can you make your money from some other part of the value chain?

Reach out to customers, non-customers and commentators

What are they happy with? Why don't they use your product? How do they use it in practice? What are they unhappy with? What do they think of advertising, experience, service and quality? Are they ready for a change? Are people talking about a gap in the marketplace? Has anyone innovated in a big way and failed?

Create new business models

Your business model is your approach to creating value in any particular strategic space *and* how you intend turning that value into revenue. Prior to the internet revolution there were many different business models but they were not often spoken about.

The internet has allowed entrepreneurs and innovators to find new ways of delivering services and receiving payments for those services. You should write down how you are going to provide value to a particular market segment with a specific value and supply chain. Then you can start to play with the accepted business models in your strategic group to see if there are opportunities for innovation and enhanced strategic advantage.

Success

Getting a sense of the dynamic, rules and positioning is the initial point of looking at strategic groups. You want to know who you are up against. You want to know the rules so that you know when to keep them and when to break them.

You want to know the rhythm and shape of change so that you can get a sense of timing. If there are frequent revolutions, you have to be ready to react, adapt and get ahead of the strategic group if possible. If there hasn't been an innovation in the past hundred years then you can afford to take your time and also consider how best to educate customers and suppliers in your space.

You will be getting value out of the process if you understand strategic groups but the next step is to simplify that knowledge down into strategic choices. If you are the one making the decision then there has to be a decision to be made. This may be about a specific choice between products or it may be a more directional choice about strategic spaces. Even if you're not going to make the decisions, you want to be able to describe the choices available.

If you can anticipate and interpret the strategic moves of others you have gained something worthwhile. If you can creatively find ways of producing cumulative (or disruptive) benefits for your company, that's even better. This may come from redefining the nature of your product, service or market. It can also include creating new market boundaries.

Strategists' measures of success

→ Traditional dimensions of competition are identified.

→ Strategic groups are understood across traditional and non-traditional dimensions.

→ Strategic spaces (and their dynamics) are explored and discussed.

→ Opportunities (gaps) and threats across strategic spaces are identified and explored.

→ You have working scenarios for growth within and outside traditional strategic groups.

Pitfalls

Ignoring the traditional strategic group is dangerous. It can leave you without any understanding of how they are likely to respond to your strategic choices regarding price, service, quality and performance. You can lose out in the day-to-day decisions about how to compete and how to look after your customers.

It is also dangerous to be limited by the boundaries and behaviour of the traditional strategic group. New entrants can create new rules. And existing competitors can prepare strategy and products that remove the need for your whole company.

Strategists' checklist

■ Always take the time to understand the strategic groups that surround your company and your strategy. Who are your main competitors and how do they compare? You need to know the answers to these questions. If you don't – find out or hire someone who already knows.

■ Be flexible and creative in looking at what may happen next in your strategic group. Look for sweet spots in available strategic space. Think about how the strengths of the organisation match the demands of any new space you find (see page 215) and what to do about it.

■ Use the various tools in the toolkit creatively to try to find effective strategic actions and potentially attractive strategic spaces.

Related ideas

Clayton Christensen, in his book *The Innovator's Prescription*, argues for the power of Business Model Innovation (BMI) as a way of changing the rules and disrupting a strategic group or even a whole industry. Often supported by technological advances, the BMI changes the source of money or value, leaving competitors isolated.

More recently, *Business Model Generation*, by Alexander Osterwalder and Yves Pigneur, introduced the Business Model Canvas as one method for pulling these various options together.

A key difference between innovation and strategy is that innovation is, by definition, about new ideas, while strategy is not necessarily new. A key similarity between innovation and strategy is that they both involve potential for failure, and so both require adaptation and learning to succeed and keep succeeding.

At a general level, business model innovation is a deliberate attempt to wrap strategy around new ideas for delivering and capturing value. And it's already become an official priority for a growing majority of large organisations. They don't wait for external shocks to force new adaptations. Instead, people actively look for ways of disrupting existing markets and competitors. This, as Luis Martins of McCombs School of Business points out, requires a change in mental schemas. You'll need an internal shock led by imagination, curiosity, playfulness and ambition.

Growing your business (again and again)

Strategy isn't something you do once and then follow forever. If you want to grow you're going to need to keep looking at your strategy to see if it still fits. And even if it fits you'll need to figure out new actions that keep the strategy working as you grow.

Frequency: Quarterly.
Key participants: You with your organisation.
Strategy rating: ****

Oracle began with an idea and three people. Over the next thirty-five years, it captured 50 per cent of the relational database market and grew to nearly $40 billion in annual revenue. To keep growing has required a clever mix of strategies. This included calling its original product version 2.0 to encourage customers to believe in its reliability and hiring the disgraced ex-CEO of a key rival to bring in vital expertise and contacts. And when the original growth curve levelled off, it continued with strategic acquisitions of companies so that it can create new sources of growth. While also making strategic acquisitions of talent (hiring people) it needs to understand and drive forward its delivery of its strategic mission: hardware and software engineered to work together. More recently it has launched a seemingly impossible price war with Amazon for fast-growing cloud services (see page 98). This mission has – like everything else – been evolved in pursuit of eternal growth.

Objective

Organisations go through life stages. They experience life events. You take your first baby steps, experience temper tantrums, adolescent acne and teenage angst. There are the midlife crises.

And ultimately, if no one does anything to stop it – there is corporate decline and eventual death.

Yet organisations are not limited by age. They can survive and then they can grow forever. They can outlive the people who started them. And they can overcome the series of growth crises by being continually renewed and reborn.

Strategy is about adapting to circumstances to achieve particular objectives. And so, as circumstances change over time the strategy, or the particular approaches taken to turn the strategy into action, must change.

Your strategy has to be a perpetual process rather than a dead document. It also has to see further ahead than today's events. It should be anticipating the challenges, threats and opportunities of next month, quarter, year and decade.

Context

Everything has a lifecycle. There are product lifecycles. There are industry lifecycles. The strategic group you are part of has a lifecycle. So will your organisation. And so will your strategy.

First there is introduction (or birth), then growth, maturity and finally decline. Each stage has expected threats, opportunities and standard responses. You don't have to follow those standard responses but it makes sense to know about them, to know the rules before you break them.

Part of this is shaped by demand for your products. At the start of the business you need to find resources and talent. Then you will work hard to get attention. Your strategy will reach out to innovators and visionaries who want to try new things. Your marketing will have to attract the attention of those who create trends and hunt cool.

The next step is to attempt to jump the chasm between innovators and the early adopters who are the first part of the mass market. This often involves changing marketing and also ramping up the organisation to deal with greater demand. Early success must be followed by a consolidation.

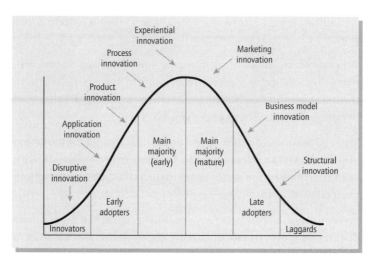

Lifecycles of strategy and innovation

This consolidation and increasing maturity is a natural part of the company and product lifecycle. The process also leads naturally to a new crisis. Each stage creates problems and each problem requires a solution. The solutions are a mixture of standard responses and new innovations.

As a strategist your job is to see the bigger picture so that you can create strategy that will shape the future. You can use these models to anticipate what is likely to happen to your organisation over time.

- What stage has your organisation reached?
- What stage has your industry reached?
- What stage have your products and services reached?
- What crisis has your organisation faced? What will be next?

The priority is to survive. For this you have to take standard actions. But the objective is to grow more successful. And this is often the most effective way of surviving – to look past survival as a goal and embrace growth as a goal.

- How has your organisation grown in the past?
- How fast will it grow if current trends and competition continue?

■ What is the organisation's engine for growth?

■ Who does it need to help it keep growing?

■ Which organisations, markets and products could help growth?

Challenge

Continued growth is a series of growth curves with new curves starting before the ultimate decline of the organisation. The internal challenges of the organisation have to be sorted to find new products that meet the needs of new and existing customers. And all while dealing with competitors.

It's the role of strategy to transcend these problems. You will need practical solutions to specific problems. You will also need imaginative solutions that will inspire and engage employees, suppliers and customers. Strategy is the combination of new vision that is sufficiently novel to re-energise desire and sufficiently credible to be believed.

Do the various parts of the organisation and strategy fit?

You want a strategy that fits the demands of a growing market. If you are not in a growing market you need to figure out how to turn that around or find a new market. You want an organisation with the skills necessary to put your strategy into practice. If you have the wrong skills and wrong people then your strategy may still fail because it cannot move from theory into action.

Work through the logic of your strategy and then into the practical reality. Look for contradictions between what you want to accomplish and the way you are organised.

Does your organisation need to be split?

Even if you have the right parts in the right places in a general sense, it is still possible for them to move too slowly. It's also possible for them to change too slowly when new change arrives.

Sometimes the corporate functions become overwhelmed dealing with the demands of planning for a complex organisation.

In response it brings in more and more rules, and more and more layers of rule makers and enforcers. This makes the problem worse. To free the talent and effectiveness of the field the only way is to increase the autonomy of the field. You need to empower, decentralise and unclog the corporate arteries.

Does your organisation have enough constructive conflict?

You need just enough disunity for progress. Too much unity and there are no new ideas, no criticism and no improvement. Too much disunity and there is never any action because people can't agree for long enough to get anything done.

As a strategist, observe the level of conflict. Look at whether it is open, transparent and constructive. Or is it closed, hidden, with smart people biting their tongues and keeping their best ideas quiet?

Has your organisation learned to transcend contradictions and conflict?

One of the valuable roles creative strategy can play is to overcome the sources of conflict. First you identify areas of disagreement – which is easier if people are being open about it. You also look for contradictions in the way you run your business and the strategy you are meant to be following. Finally, you look for clever ways of overcoming those conflicts and contradictions.

This process is never perfect, and it's often messy, but it is the only way of figuring out what to do next and engaging people with the problem-solving process *and* the solution implementation activities.

Success

You'll understand where you are on various lifecycle models. You will know if your organisation is young, middle-aged, vibrant or in decline. There will also be a clear view of the growth stage of your industry and the products and services you offer. Each may be at a different stage and these will overlap.

To make practical (and strategic) use of your knowledge, you will examine the typical crisis points related to your place in various lifecycles. You will know, for instance, whether your products are new born and innovative in an industry that is mature and declining (see Part six: *The Strategy Book* toolkit).

Ideally, you will develop strategic responses to your place in the corporate lifecycle to identify new paths of strategic renewal. You will look for new growth curves that can be started early enough to replace declining products. And you will try to identify whole new curves that will take the organisation to new levels of growth as a whole.

You will look specifically at what needs to be changed in order to avoid falling off a growth cliff and accepting terminal decline. This is valuable work. Many organisations remain in denial of chronic threats. Others recognise the threats but cannot see a way out, while certain organisations see the way out but cannot figure out how to make the changes necessary to get there.

Strategists' measures of success

→ Know where you are on the industry, product and company lifecycle.

→ Understand the timescales of any particular threat related to your stage of growth.

→ Familiarise yourself with the standard challenges and solutions related to each stage of the lifecycles.

→ Use *The Strategy Book* creatively to produce strategic responses to the threats and opportunities of growth.

→ Identify effective ways of making changes sufficient to accomplish growth.

Pitfalls

It is easy to assume that whatever you did to solve the last growth problem will be the answer to solving the next growth problem. The reverse is often true. For example, the challenges of growth require structure and process, but the challenges of structure require creativity and autonomy. This creates danger for the organisation because previous answers will rarely work. Each new challenge demands rapid learning on the part of existing employees and leaders. It may also need people with experience of whatever challenge you now have.

Trying to create strategy for growth may be slowed down (or even sabotaged) by those who feel they have more to lose in the brave new world. Imagine being the leader of a department that is branded as the 'cash cow' or the 'dog'. They may see no reason to give up resources to fund the growth of rising stars. Or they may not want to allow an upstart to cannibalise their products or services.

This creates a tough situation where the organisation knows what it should do but doesn't do it. Blockbuster, for example, knew that rental by mail and video streaming was the future but they just couldn't bring themselves to make the necessary changes.

The same was true in the boardrooms of Ford, GM and Chrysler. They knew that competition was coming from Honda, Nissan and Toyota but could not make the necessary changes. You have to turn the long emergency into something more compelling. Use urgency for momentum.

Strategists' checklist

- Identify your company's stage in the corporate lifecycle.

- Use the strategist's toolkit to locate your key products and services on their own lifecycles.

- Consider creatively how to head off the next decline via strategic renewal of products, services and people.

- Use scenario-planning techniques to think forward. Work together with other teams to imagine various futures and consider your options (see page 183).

■ List areas that are blocking changes that have already been identified. Think about how these can be overcome to allow growth to continue.

Related ideas

Burgelman and Grove (ex-CEO of Intel) propose that continued growth requires the leader to move between autonomy and control at different times. Their article used the term 'Let Chaos Reign, Then Rein in Chaos' to express their method (see page 209).

You can enjoy the comfort of exploiting what you already have, but you risk falling behind more imaginative competitors. Or you can brave the discomfort of exploring what is unproven, but you risk spending time and money on things you don't know will ever work. It's a tough choice.

Recent work by Ming Piao and Edward Zaja is a good reminder that smart strategists can make more nuanced choices. Repetitive exploitation, they argue, really does get in the way of new ideas. But exploitation that is incremental, or iterative, can allow a really clever way of getting value from new ideas without betting the company.

Going global without going broke

There are immense opportunities for the internationally minded corporation. All it takes is the strategic decision to go beyond being a one-country business. Of course, you might expand too far, too fast, and regret it. But you have the chance to become a global brand.

Frequency: Review regularly and opportunistically.
Key participants: You and your boss.
Strategy rating: ****

Vodafone was the first mobile phone company in the United Kingdom. The CEO worked with US contacts to develop its original technology. He kept the company looking outside national boundaries for new opportunities. As a result, Vodafone also made the first international roaming call with partners from Finland. Vodafone recognised the choice between growing and being dominated. It uses global reach to compete with new rivals, like Apple and Google.

Vodafone expanded globally through partnership and acquisition. It did deals, and bought competitors to find more customers for its core mobile products. It sold subsidiaries to fund investment in faster-growing countries. It became one of the biggest companies and most valuable brands in the world with half a billion customers in thirty countries. This growth was made possible by the international outlook of its leadership who created a global portfolio.

Objective

The world is a big place. And because it's a big place there will always be more opportunities for growth outside your country than inside it. If you limit your ambition to the national market you will never reach the potential of your business. You can be the most admired company in your own backyard, city or region but that will stop you achieving a lot of very attractive goals.

- How could global expansion provide better opportunities?
- Could you avoid some threats by expanding globally?
- What are the most effective global expansion strategies?
- Why would expanding globally fail? What could stop you?

Whatever business you are in, there is the chance that a bigger competitor will arrive that will make it difficult for you to survive. This bigger competitor usually becomes bigger by doing business in more places than you. It has extra resources. It can hire more people. It can hire more talent. It has the benefits of size on its side. It is comparing itself to the best in the world, not the best in the country. It has higher standards, more ideas and more ambition.

There are threats in every market. Some of these threats are reduced by expanding outside of your national constraints, in part because you are growing bigger – taking the competitive fight to other countries before they bring it to you.

Context

You don't have to be big to be international – you just have to do business with someone in another country. Global is something else.

Traditionally the biggest trading groups have been the USA, Japan and the EU. They do the most international trade and have the most global brands. Many of the examples in this book are from those three because they got biggest and most global ahead of other countries and continents.

The bigger picture is changing. China is now the world's biggest economy. The fastest-growing economies are all in the developing world. And – more significantly – they are moving from just supplying goods to global brands to developing (or buying) their own international brands.

The developed markets are the biggest; the developing markets are the fastest growing. Either way, the real action is outside of any particular country. You want to plug your company's growth into world growth.

Challenge

There is no single guaranteed global strategy that will win. Part of it is almost accidental. You need to be looking outwards and making the most of global opportunities that come your way. Coca-Cola, McDonalds and several other global brands followed their armed forces during and after wars.

Getting it right in your own country first plays a part. Becoming a real national player (like Vodafone) can be a huge help in generating enough income, expertise and reputation to be able to fund your international expansion. Walmart had such advantages in supply chain management and economies of scale that it was able to buy success in a number of other countries.

But national excellence is not the whole story. There are numerous examples of nationally dominant companies that do not become global brands. Sometimes, they do not try – a lack of international ambition and experience stops the attempt before it starts. Sometimes, they do not succeed – they are unlucky or try to force their approach on international markets without making the necessary changes.

Walmart has become an international company. It is one of the world's largest companies. It is one of the world's most valuable brands. But despite its advantages it is not really a global company or a global brand. In many national markets it has found it very difficult either to get started or get growing. In the UK, it found an ideal partner – ASDA – who had based their growth on an idealistic understanding of the Walmart Way. But Walmart has made little progress in many countries (such as South America), and in some (such as Japan) it has struggled because of a failure to adapt.

Despite the challenges, if you have something unique, or at least valuable, in your home market then it's possible that there will be demand for it elsewhere. It may even be the case that what is commonplace in your home market is unique in the rest of the world. Germans appear to very good at building luxury cars: Audi, Mercedes and BMW. The Japanese appear to have key skills in creating consumer electronics: Sony, Toshiba and Nintendo. The Italians are phenomenal at sports cars: Lamborghini, Maserati and Ferrari.

Success

Just the act of deciding to go global seems to change the likelihood of strategic success. This worked for countries that decided to explore the world, bringing back wealth and knowledge. And it also works for business leaders who decide to explore. They may bring back great ideas – like the Red Bull founders who saw an idea in South-East Asia and then nurtured it into a global brand. They may also capture the imagination of their own people and the general public – often through momentum itself.

When considering your global strategy, there are many approaches. One is to carefully understand the nature of globalisation facing your company.

- How globalised is your industry?
- How globalised is your country?
- How globalised is your company already?

If you are facing competition from global competitors who are also growing fast elsewhere in the world, then the case for going global has become urgent. At the very least you need to understand your options. If you decide to stay national or regional, then you should know why. You should also examine what you will do about the big competitors now – and particularly in the future.

You should examine the level of experience you have with growing and managing a global company. If you don't have that kind of experience and knowledge then it may reduce your confidence with international expansion. There are certain practical steps that benefit from first-hand experience. And there are relationships that are invaluable to building an international network.

You can benefit from a global strategy in many different ways. You can try to find new markets for your existing (standard or slightly modified) products. You can look for new sources of production to manufacture better or at a lower cost. And you can use your existing resources to develop new products for new markets. (Use the growth grid on page 185 and other tools globally.)

There are trends that support this move. Markets are starting to behave in relatively similar ways to (more or less) global standards and norms. And, according to some criteria, customers are also becoming similar (not the same). They are more likely to share traits across segments (or tribes) than within a particular country. This is not an absolute rule but it's helpful.

To move to a global strategy greatly increases some of the complexity. There are new laws, customs, relationships, customer behaviours and – usually – language. This last point explains why some global strategies start within zones of shared language and even culture. But it's easy to be fooled by the similarities rather than noticing the differences.

Strategists' measures of success

➤ You know which countries are growing fastest and which are largest.

➤ You understand which countries are most important for your growth.

➤ The company has a global strategy (even if it is very, very small).

➤ Your strategy has an international outlook for knowledge and expansion.

➤ Real success is measured by actually expanding globally.

Pitfalls

The most obvious pitfall is failing to cope with the differences (big or small) between countries. Knowing what to change and what to keep standard is a problem. It is dangerous to expand too quickly, particularly if your company makes financial commitments that are long term. Try to keep things flexible enough to be able to learn lessons and change. Another mistake is to assume there is only one way and speed of going global. You can start slow in just one country through a partner or go fast by acquiring companies all over the world.

Strategists' checklist

- Understand advantages you may have over competitors in different countries. Are there any strengths of your country that will put you in a winning position if you export or open up for business internationally?

- How could increasing the size of your company's operations provide you with advantages? These economies of scale and scope may allow you advantages that put you ahead of national competitors in many or all countries. This is particularly true if you are among the first in your strategic group and market to adopt a global expansion strategy.

- Consider the advantages of a global strategy for learning and innovation. Even if you don't open up premises in other countries you can open up your mind to the partnerships and sources of knowledge. And once you have done that then opportunities to expand products and services, particularly via the internet, will become more apparent.

Related ideas

Christopher Bartlett and Sumantra Ghoshal argue throughout their work, including *Managing Across Borders*, that there are three key tasks, or needs, of global strategy: *Need for efficiency* – creating a dispersed, interdependent and specialised value chain; *Need for national responsiveness* – moving to federal structure with different units; and *Need for innovation* – developing simultaneous central, local and global learning.

Knowing what you can do best

Every company is a collection of skills and resources. Every company combines those skills and resources in unique ways with processes, technology and culture. And this, combined with specific decisions in a specific marketplace, leads to performance.

Frequency: Regularly and annually.
Key participants: You and your organisation.
Strategy rating: Strategy6

Google grows when it does what it does best, and its official strategy makes that clear. It seeks to 'organize the world's information and make it universally accessible and useful', and it's great at doing exactly that. It successfully revolutionised search; not just search for text but for video, images, audio, books and news. Its ability in search allowed it to understand (and benefit from) the value of YouTube.

But whenever Google strays into areas it does not understand it stalls. For example, it has launched Facebook competitors several times without success. This is the strategic thinking behind Google's new holding company, Alphabet. This is somewhere to become the best at drones, home-automation, self-driving cars and space-travel. It's money wasted if they invest in new markets without becoming better. It's money invested if Google becomes the best in those new markets.

Objective

The opportunity is to understand your skills and resources better so that you can focus on your strengths. You can deliver products and services better (or more originally) than anyone else. You can discover what no one else can do.

In a sense you are trying to find an 'unfair' advantage, something you can deliver best because of your particular combination of knowledge, relationships, brand and resources (see page 62).

- What can you do really well?
- What can you do that competitors can't?
- How can you use your unique abilities and skills to deliver what customers really want?

Give this a lot of thought. Not just once but often. Don't just try to copy what a competitor is doing. Think about the way you work and how that might be difficult to copy. Then consider how to exaggerate the benefits of what you do.

Toyota decided to compete with Mercedes in the luxury car segment. But instead of copying the way that Mercedes produced luxury cars, they used their own unique production system to produce cars faster, at a much lower cost, and of better quality. They knew what they were good at and used these capabilities as a strategy to compete with the luxury car knowledge of Mercedes.

Ideally, you will find something that is difficult to copy (inimitable), durable, difficult to substitute, easy to make money from and obviously superior from a customer's point of view.

Context

Strategy is not just about actions and opportunities. It is about figuring out how opportunities relate to your strengths and weaknesses. If you can't do something that is necessary to the success of your plan, then your plan will not succeed unless you can fill the gap.

Alternatively you can stay with plans that depend on strengths that you already have. This is particularly powerful when your strengths are relative to others in the same competitive space. It is even more powerful if you create strategy from an overlap between strengths and opportunity.

- How can you make your strategic gap into a strategic stretch?
- How can you build from where you are to where you want to be?

This kind of strategic stretch can be very attractive but is only likely to be successful if the gap is understood. More specifically, it is more likely to be understood if the strategic stretch can be made more or less naturally from one position of strength to an extended position of strength.

Challenge

If you do need to fill gaps, some of the gap filling can come from learning. Some weaknesses can be remedied by training. Other weaknesses can be addressed by recruiting people with the experience and skills you think you need. But there are difficulties with each of these.

Because gaining significantly new abilities is difficult and costly it's important to ask the following questions:

- Is the opportunity worth the effort and risk of gaining new capabilities and strengths?
- Are the threats sufficient to overcome embedded weaknesses?

Learning takes time. And even dedicated attempts at learning – particularly at corporate level – can struggle to move much past the core competencies of your organisation. If you are to embark on learning to extend what you are best at then that learning will require challenges to how you think. And this challenge has to extend from the top throughout the organisation – with external support and embedded internal efforts.

Recruiting can be a shortcut to gaining knowledge, yet if the recruited people are a minority or are not able to be understood then their success will be restricted. Many companies have hired experts only for their expertise to be blunted by the existing biases of the organisation. Strengths can get in the way because it's seemingly more effective to do what you are best at.

Success

The key to success is a flexible, clear understanding of the strengths of your organisation – what you do best – and how they relate to the strategic opportunities that are available to you.

Don't worry if this all seems difficult to get your head around. The whole area of core competencies and the Resource-Based View (RBV) has vexed managers and academics for decades. The difficulty is what makes the effort worthwhile.

It is the creativity with which you use those fundamental strengths that will enable or limit your growth. Can you see the bigger picture related to your strengths? Can you pull something fundamental out of the collections of CVs, skills and resources that your organisation has available? What would it be easier for you to do than your competitors? Where would it be worth making the expensive effort to gain new capabilities?

Success also means understanding the limitations of your current strengths. What are the dangers of staying within your ability comfort zone? There is a risk of a kind of capability caricature where you only do what you have done before and where you exaggerate the parts that you are good at to the detriment of what you don't understand.

Strategists' measures of success

→ You know what has brought you success in the past.

→ There is understanding about what you are best at doing.

→ You have a sense of the limits to your strengths.

→ Opportunity spaces for your strengths have been explored.

→ Strategic plans are examined for gaps between strengths and weaknesses.

Pitfalls

Understanding what you are best at is not meant to stop you learning. New skills and knowledge are still needed. The search for what you are best at can be confused with just looking for what you have done well and repeating it.

If you stop learning or restrict your strategy to what has worked before you constrain your future growth. You will also impair your ability to adapt to new challenges and opportunities. The aim is to understand what you are great at in a more flexible, holistic way.

Strategists' checklist

- Explore your strengths in detail, but always look for the essence of your strengths. Work with your colleagues to sum up your core strengths in a clear way. Imagine that you are writing an advertisement for your abilities rather than for your products or services. What is the slogan?

- Use SWOT analysis (see page 167) in a more creative way to examine the links between opportunities and strengths. Look for links that would allow you to follow opportunities more effectively than competitors.

- Consider the costs of acquiring new capabilities. Don't just believe that ambition to succeed in areas you are weak in is enough. Try to learn from past attempts to extend the brand or the company into new areas.

- Be open about what your core competencies are and what they can become. Is it your ability to learn? Is it your power to complete tasks quickly? Can your ability to hire be a core strength? Each part of the value chain can be a source of competitive advantage, so figure out how they can combine to deliver that advantage.

Related ideas

Jay Barney, Professor of Strategic Management at the University of Utah, is closely associated with the Resource-Based View (RBV). He argues that collections of resources and capabilities can be made more difficult to copy. These inimitable resources can form the basis of sustainable competitive advantage if strategy is shaped around them.

part

five

Making your strategy work

The power in strategy is in shaping your future. This means that to be useful, strategy has to work in the real world. Many strategies are created for a fictional world where simply writing down objectives is enough to achieve them. It is a world where the commands of distant executives are instantly obeyed and where every assumption in the strategy stays true forever.

The skilled strategist is not content with just creating a strategy document. The aim of the skilled strategist is to shape the future, so they are interested in how to make their strategies work. Part of this is about the way strategy is created. The whole process can be designed to increase the real-world value of the ideas *and* increase engagement with the strategy.

What will happen is a mixture of what you intended and what emerges from what people actually do (including what they do best). Your strategy cannot see every threat and every opportunity that will arise between one year and the next and it cannot see every level of the hierarchy.

Your strategy process will be more effective if it includes more people and if it thinks more rigorously about different scenarios in the future. You should consider how changes happen and how to create strategy that works with human behaviour (and for the good of individuals) rather than against it.

Many things will go wrong before you get to any particular end goal. The goal itself may have to change for the organisation to survive or grow. The organisation will face many different crises of growth or decline. And it is the role of strategy to prepare the organisation to better respond to these challenges.

Managing your strategy process

Strategy is not really a solo sport – even if you're the CEO. At its most effective, it involves people and knowledge at all levels, inside and outside the organisation. Part of this is organising strategy creation, measurement and implementation in clever ways that work.

Frequency: Monthly and annually.
Key participants: You and your organisation.
Strategy rating: Strategy6

The CEO of GE decided the company should grow organically two or three times faster than GDP. It's been described as an audacious goal. To achieve it, they redesigned their strategy process. Instead of annual, they wanted continual. Instead of complexity, they wanted simplicity. Real-time employee appraisements evolved to match the new rhythm of the business – and the world. The aim was to create more ambitious, more insightful strategic approaches to growing. And then to make those strategies work in the real world more effectively than ever.

The process had to engage people and empower them to move faster. It took about two years to work out a six-part process for creating and executing. It was custom made for GE people by GE people. The process is circular with no obvious starting point. Each component (customers, innovation, technology, commercial, globalisation and leaders) reinforces overall strategic effort.

Objective

There are many different strategy management processes. Small (and large) companies may have no formal process. They figure out what they are doing as they go along. Large (and small) corporations may have a formal strategy planning cycle that starts three to six months before the start of the next financial year.

In this formal process, individual departments are expected to create plans which are emailed up the hierarchy. These plans contribute to the corporate strategy, which is then emailed down the hierarchy again. At this point, some kind of negotiation about resources and financial goals often starts and the strategy is more or less followed, or more or less ignored, depending on the traditions of the organisation.

Some organisations start at the top and just tell people what they have to achieve, while others try to involve everyone because they will need everyone's ideas and help in making the strategy work. For some companies, it's superficial – with few people even aware of what's been agreed. For others it can be painfully detailed as political games are played while bureaucracy strangles any creativity that was in the original plans.

Ideally, the strategy process should engage the hearts and minds of the whole company continually throughout the year. The strategy is the company, and the company is the strategy. It follows that imaginative and knowledgeable involvement with a fluid, dynamic strategy process is helpful.

Context

There are several parts of a strategy management process. You may use all of these or just some of them. The important thing is to be aware of them and then to be able to start shaping a process that makes an effective contribution to the performance of the organisation.

The traditional strategy planning cycle often starts with a review at the highest level of progress made against the previous year's plan. In reality, this review has been made all the way through the year – performance is usually cumulative although there are often surprises near the end.

This is always strategic in the sense that it is based on the overall views of the top management. But it is often *not* strategic because it doesn't consider the bigger picture. It often doesn't think about the state of the company, its position in the market, where this is likely to lead, given performance and trends, or whether the mission, goals, purpose or sources of competitive advantage should be changed.

There is a tendency to just roll-over the strategy from one year to the next. Fairly straightforward projections are made about what will happen in the future. These are applied to new goals for the New Year. They tend to be adjusted up if the pressure is on from shareholders. They may be adjusted down if trends appear to be against easy growth.

Sometimes the detail of the plans is *middle up*, either gathered from individual function or business heads, then stuck together into a single document and redistributed with a few tweaks. Or the detail of the plans is gathered from goals set at the top of the organisation, communicated to the middle and then negotiated before a final agreement is made about goals, investment, plans and remuneration. Either way planning is piecemeal and goals are a compromise.

Challenge

The problems with traditional planning processes are numerous. Not enough time is spent imaginatively examining the strategy. The existing strategy is accepted without testing assumptions, desirability or credibility.

Find enough time for the executive team (and various levels below) to look at the bigger, strategic picture. Not just a day but a week. Not just once a year but two, three, four times a year. Get a talented facilitator in to make the strategic time more effective, creative and enjoyable. Even monthly and weekly meetings can be made more strategic. You can turn agenda time into thinking time that can outwit competitors and find real competitive advantage.

Accelerate and deepen strategy process with the help of many more people inside and outside the organisation. This doesn't have to be laborious. You can cut down the number of months the whole process takes by involving people in a focused number of strategy events. Schedule them between the executive team meetings. Explore the strategy and different scenarios. Examine lessons from strategy implementation and apply those lessons to your strategic plan.

Co-create a strategy model to be debated by your organisation. The decisions are still made clearly but they can be made into a real debate with involvement from the whole company. If you can simplify the strategy into a model that makes sense to everyone then they can contribute to making it work. If it has been created with them then it has meaning, so they are emotionally engaged with *their* strategy for winning. Paint it (and progress) up on walls, on floors – let people know.

This way is better because it supports dynamic strategy. And dynamic strategy is better adapted to the needs of your dynamic competitive environment. The whole organisation, processes and culture contribute. They can improve the speed and intelligence of what you learn and how you respond.

Success

You will move away from a slow, dull, once-a-year bargaining process for agreeing financial goals. You will develop a fast, engaging, continual learning process for creating strategy that wins by creating cumulative competitive advantage.

Goals are still necessary. And measurement systems and financial controls have their role to play. But avoid making them more hard work than they are worth. Focus your efforts on encouraging the kind of strategic thinking and action that creates and delivers competitive advantage.

Make sure that you know what success looks like for *your* strategy. How will you know that you are making progress towards accomplishment of your mission? How will you know that your strategy is working? How will the contribution of groups and individuals to the strategy be measured? Strategy is meant to move you in the most effective way from means to ends. If you don't know what success looks like you will not be able to learn from what does happen.

Strategists' measures of success

→ You have a process that links each layer of strategy with each level of hierarchy.

→ Everyone in the company knows what success of the strategy looks like.

→ There is a balanced scorecard for measuring strategy and managing progress.

→ Considerable time for learning, thinking, reviewing and creating strategy is found.

→ The strategy management process engages and prepares people to contribute.

Pitfalls

Strategy processes can become too vague so that they create more problems than they solve. They can leave people feeling unsure what the direction is and how they will know they are making progress. It's also possible for the strategy management process to provide little commitment or understanding. People can feel clear about how they will be rewarded but not about how what they do will contribute to the bigger picture. Or why they should care.

Strategists' checklist

■ Write down (or draw) the existing strategy management process. If you don't have a formal process, write down how the goals in the company are decided. Your process may be very complex or almost non-existent. Either way you need to know what it is so you can consider whether it is fit for purpose. Only then can you redesign to create a better solution.

- Make your strategy process about strategy. Most strategy processes involve very little strategy. The real strategy is in the heads of people, while the process is all about agreeing financial goals based on expected performance. Introduce strategic thinking and start to shape the future.

- Involve more people in the strategy process. Ask people in the organisation what kind of problems they are facing and what opportunities they can see. Use those ideas as you organise your first really strategic planning session.

- Create momentum. Treat your strategy process as a strategy campaign. Start with low-key conversations that ask strategy-type questions. Use the questions in this book to begin (and improve) the strategic conversation in your company.

- Build towards a new-style strategy planning session. This would preferably be a couple of days away from the office.

- Plan your first days around the key strategy questions (see page 165). And then build up material and activities that allow you to have a knowledgeable and enjoyable time examining the questions.

- Consider investing in expert facilitation. It's worth paying for people who know what they are doing. This is the future of the business and so should be valuable. There are people at different price points so look around to find someone you can trust and who can move you ahead.

- Create a strategy calendar for your company. Start with at least a few sessions that build up to the creation of an agreed strategy for the year. And then follow up to assess progress, opportunities, threats and new ideas.

- Make this book the basis of increasing the strategic thinking in your organisation. Introduce the subject of innovation as a way of improving your ability to find sources of competitive advantage.

Related ideas

Kaplan and Norton argue for the creation of an 'office of strategy management' in every corporation. This function would help strategy work by fulfilling a leadership role. Instead of just supporting a planning process, this strategy team helps lead the process from creation to execution.

Valuable research, by Markus Menz and Christine Scheef at the Institute of Management at the University of St. Gallen in Switzerland, shows that more complex organisations are more likely to have a chief strategy officer. It also suggests that just having a chief strategy officer makes no difference to success or failure.

Smart strategists learn that if there is a secret to successful strategic thinking and action, it's not about merely having an office or an officer. It's much more likely to be about how well the strategy process – formal and informal - helps people in the organisation to successfully adapt to the environment (see page 225).

Meetings for strategic minds

A great strategy meeting is a meeting of minds. You want people thinking and talking openly about progress and aspirations. You will have a mixture of heads in the clouds and feet on the ground. There is no one best way but here is a good starting point.

Frequency: Regularly.
Key participants: Various groups.
Strategy rating: ****

The previous CEO of Disney began a series of 'crazy idea' breakfast meetings. At each meeting, everyone was invited to discuss the direction, performance and strategy of the company. The main way this was done was through stories and ideas. People would share stories that brought strategy to life. Stories about what they wanted strategy to be, ways they were delivering and what wasn't working. These stories allowed people outside the room to be represented in the strategy discussion. And they joined creative strategy and action levels of the company powerfully together.

Now taught as an approach by the Disney Institute, this approach to creative strategy meetings spread far beyond the breakfast meetings. Bringing strategy to life became a tradition that survived and developed under the next CEO. Disney believes this style of strategic conversation encourages teaching, sharing, approachability, hope and empathy. The new CEO runs a weekly strategy lunch that has enabled talented people from the Disney Parks, Animation, Pixar, Marvel and Star Wars teams to share insights. They stay independent, yet combine strategically, with record-breaking results.

Objective

You want a meeting of minds (not a mindless meeting). The bad news is that people have often fallen into bad habits. The good news is that people want great meetings and very rarely (if ever) have attended any. They are waiting for something worthwhile and want you to succeed.

Get enough time for the session so that you will be able to make progress with strategy questions. If it's your first new-style session, get a couple of days together. Stay in a hotel. Make it feel like the start of something important. Done right, it will be a hugely valuable turning point in the history of the company. You will be shaping the future of everyone involved.

Context

Timing is important to strategy *and* to strategy meetings. People seek an agenda so they have structure but they can then use structure to avoid really engaging with the substance of the discussion. So the overall objectives serve as a lightweight structure without letting people drift off from the discussion.

For the same reason, as soon as initial objectives are accomplished, move on with additional objectives. And develop discussions from ideas to practical steps that can be followed up with names, dates and criteria for achievement.

It makes sense to confirm the schedule for the year during each meeting, particularly when you are moving from traditional (or no) strategy thinking to dynamic strategy management.

Limiting time for making decisions, or recommendations, is also engaging for many participants who are used to clock watching. It brings out the healthy, fun, competitive side of people. And it ensures that time is used effectively, so that people want to come back and engage with future sessions.

Challenge

Before the session get people prepared and engaged. Start conversations about strategy long before any formal meetings. Dynamic strategy is something continuous so treat it as such.

Questions

Ask all participants to look at the basic (powerful) strategy questions (see page 165). Get them to think about the questions for your company. Have them write down some answers. Ask them to write down the company or brand they admire the most.

Session organisers

Gather operating facts, employee survey results, financial results and projections. Look for information about key competitors. This provides information for the group to refer to, as and when it's important.

Warm up

Get people thinking even if it's a little painful to start with. The value of warming up is that it allows people to get into thinking mode. This is unusual for people who are used to going around the circle of death, reporting in turn on what they have been doing.

Choose and complete a creative activity

These can be elaborate or simple. I've seen juggling, paper plane making, quizzes, dancing, yoga or brain-teasers. Some people create their own warm-up activities. Some people use one of the many useful brainstorming books. Others hire entertainers or facilitators to deliver something very memorable. It can sound over the top, but new experiences are the only way of opening up minds to new thoughts – particularly if they are enjoying the process. Smart companies know it works.

If you're smart, you'll have several activities available – more than you need. And you will move to them at various points in the session to keep people awake. Even better if the activities are linked with the fundamental strategy questions that you will be answering and debating together.

Focused objectives and questions

Once people are warmed up, move to a brief discussion of the objectives of the session. What do you want to get done? No more than three to five objectives. Involve people to continue the two-way, open tone of the day.

It usually isn't the leader of the group who does this, so that the leader can be a team member or can get ready to make decisions about resources when those decisions are needed.

Project the basic questions up on the wall. Make it clear that these will frame the discussion. And that ultimately you are reviewing strategy progress and possibilities as part of improving both plans and performance.

Where are we now?

An update and overview of the main facts about the position of the organisation is a good idea. People need to have the basic information and they need to know that it's safe to talk. Ford's CEO made it clear that plain speaking was needed (see page 154). Apple's CEO said that they needed to change the world – and wanted ideas for doing so.

Where could we go?

This is the group's chance to get some brain food. They need new ideas from your strategic group and examples from other industries. You need to open their minds up to possibilities. Inspire them to apply new models and examples to their own work. There is no single answer to the question, but you want people ready to improve and move forward. You also want people overflowing with imaginative directions the company could take.

Where do we want to go?

This is a more practical step from the last question, yet it is still about the desirability of particular directions. You want to focus the group a little more on the direction – of all the options available – that you want to choose. Work as individuals and then as sub-groups on different directions, destinations and missions that would make sense and inspire.

Depending on the length of the meeting, it should move into action. People want to know what will happen next and you will get a better response if you move between desirable strategic objectives and believable strategic plans.

What changes have to be made?

This question is asked in light of the answers to the previous questions. The group wants to compare where the company (or team or group) is with where they want to be. Find differences between the existing position and the desired position. Get the group to write down their individual views and then bring them together into a manageable list.

How should changes be made?

Change is not automatic, even if the senior management send out emails saying that change is necessary. The group should think about two kinds of change. There are changes they can make themselves, including many decisions and anything else you just have to buy. And then there are changes that involve the behaviour and help of others.

It is the second group – the deep changes – that usually matter most. And so it is the deep changes that you should consider carefully. You should consider when and how to make changes – or ask for changes – that will engage people. You want the bodies doing things, but you really want their intellectual, emotional and creative engagement with making the strategy a success.

This is also a very practical discussion, since it eventually needs to include the detail of changes, the what, who, how and when answers that leads into something actually changing.

How should we measure progress?

Part of progress is completing the changes that you have described, but there is more. You need a relatively short set of measures that will let you know if you are getting closer to your overall strategic objectives. These measures need to be balanced enough to reflect the soft and hard aspects of what you want to achieve (see pages 197 and 201). But they also need to be precise enough to allow progress to be clear.

What next?

Any particular session will answer different questions to differing levels of detail. For the sake of momentum, it is important that each session is completed with a clear set of agreed next steps. These should contribute to the overall strategy and changes. They should be short term (days and weeks, not months or years) and they should be precise, with names and dates.

Success

The criteria for success will vary. They will depend on the amount of time that you spend on the questions, who is involved, and what stage you have reached in your strategy management process.

The group will have a good understanding of the existing position of the company and the importance and purpose of each of the questions. They will see how the questions fit together. They will have spent time exploring what they really want to achieve and how that can be made possible.

Thinking like a strategist is demanding intellectual work so they may be tired even after a very productive session. Warn them *before* the session begins that this kind of fatigue is natural. If they expect it, they will find it easier to see the progress that has been made. It is a good sign if, at some point in the middle, people feel like they are working hard.

Strategy can be a lot of intellectual and emotional fun. A great session will involve laughter. It should also involve a sense of relief, an easing of pressure as progress is made on questions. The group should be working as a group. They should be developing cross-functional habits that are more effective at answering strategic questions.

> ### Strategists' measures of success
>
> → You have scheduled strategy meetings as part of your strategy process.
>
> → Everyone taking part in the meeting has considered the strategy questions.
>
> → The strategy meeting includes thought-provoking activities.
>
> → Progress is made through the basic strategy questions.
>
> → The strategist's toolkit is used to shape and clarify discussion.
>
> → Everyone is energised and clear on the next steps by the end of the meeting.

Pitfalls

Strategy meetings involve subjects that are emotionally sensitive so they can degenerate quite easily into some kind of fight over power. This may be passive so that subtle games are played that stop progress or openness. They may also be active so that participants shout, argue or openly block.

Sometimes the group is intimidated by the most senior participant so that little meaningful discussion takes place despite willingness. Other meetings are positive but so vague that little follow-up is possible. This is frustrating for those who have invested their time and energy.

Some participants will have experiences of other strategy sessions. These may have been very uninspiring. Or they may have been part of a process that had a negative outcome – making cuts, for example. They may have contributed enthusiastically in the past and be cautious about doing so again. Or they may associate strategy with criticism and financial obsession.

Strategists' checklist

■ Think about each strategy meeting in the context of the overall position of the company (growing, flat or declining). You should have a sense of what kind of strategic challenges are faced by your company. Do some strategic thinking to understand what kind of a meeting should be held.

- Start strategic conversations before the meeting. Ideally the group should have started thinking about the questions before they get together. You can be involved with individual conversations that prepare the way for a more productive session together.

- Get enough time for the kind of meeting you need. A couple of hours to jump into all five questions can be counterproductive. You need more like a couple of days or a week. People will fight you on this point but you will make more progress if you can get the time. If you really, really can't then reduce the scope of each session to get something completed.

- Make sure each meeting ends with specific action steps so that momentum is created and maintained. People like to see progress, and you should be creating something that is more popular as time goes on.

- Relax and enjoy the session. And if you can't relax then help everyone else to relax. The style of learning is important to the effectiveness of the thinking.

Related ideas

There are many books about meetings but here is one that is good if you want to get a real idea of what is possible: *Retreats That Work: Everything You Need to Know About Planning* and *Leading Great Offsites*, by Merianne Liteman, Sheila Campbell and Jeffrey Liteman.

Managing change, making strategy work

Most strategy involves change. People will have to change something they are doing to make the strategy come to life. You need to be able to translate your strategy into actions, tasks and projects. You also need to communicate the logic and purpose of the strategy so that people get engaged with the work and are willing to help it succeed.

Frequency: Annually then continually.
Key participants: You and your organisation.
Strategy rating: Strategy6

McDonald's gained unwanted criticism for being unhealthy, dirty, slow, cheap, unethical and behind-the-times. In response, the CEO at the time, introduced a new strategy: 'Plan to Win'. It fitted onto only one page. It explained very clearly the necessary changes so everyone understood what was required. The mission changed from 'best fast-food restaurant' to 'favourite place and way to eat'.

This clear change of strategy lead to clear changes. Instead of growing locations they improved the experience. They introduced healthier food, better tasting coffee, interiors that surpassed coffee shop competitors and free Wi-Fi. Suddenly, traditional competitors were struggling to catch up. The strategy delivered eight years of sales growth. McDonald's turned around because it engaged everyone with a strategy that made sense and motivated action.

Unfortunately, the next McDonald's CEO was unable to continue with changes that were deep enough, and fast enough, to compete with a whole new generation of fast-food rivals. The menu grew ever more complex. Their reputation suffered. The competition grew profits and locations while McDonald's stalled.

The strategic direction appeared confused and defensive, until, after more than a year of declining profits, he lost his job with the McFamily. It will be for the new CEO to make his new strategy work.

Objective

Strategy involves change because it has to adapt to competitors, technology and customers. If you change the strategy but don't succeed in changing the company, then the strategy is wasted. Even worse, the company may not succeed in adapting in ways that allow it to grow and thrive.

The McDonald's example shows the importance of clarity in getting strategic changes made. The changes are made by people. People can only help if they know what is expected. And they will only help if they feel engaged with the direction of the strategy.

Context

The strategy may be correct but so boring that no one wants to read it. It may include new ideas but ideas that are not credible. It may be so complex that it takes longer to read it than do anything about it. And it may be so vague that no one knows what is expected of them if they do want to help (see page 60).

It's worth thinking about making strategy engaging before there is even a strategy in place. You could create your strategy in secret, on your own and spend months trying to sell it to the people in the company. It's far better to spend months involving everyone in creating a strategy that they understand.

- How many people can you involve in creating strategy?
- What do the people who work for you think?
- What is the simplest way of communicating the strategy?
- What would inspire the majority of people to really engage?
- How do you get the strategy beyond the superficial?

It's also important to consider the scale and nature of the change that your strategy requires. Changes might be big or small. They may involve evolution or revolution. They may be positive or negative. They may involve losing jobs or gaining jobs. The strategy might require new skills or actions. It might involve different areas of the business in different ways. It may be more externally or more internally focused.

Change comes from different perspectives. Responses to changes come from different perspectives and changes aren't going to be welcome in the same way. These tensions are what creates the attempt to make changes in the first place and will shape what eventually happens.

There may be clashes between different interest groups, or disagreements about competing plans for the future. There may be an absence of clarity about what needs to be done so that nothing clear is done. There are often winners and losers who each feel very differently about the strategy.

Challenge

There are two key challenges: how to reduce wasted effort arguing about what change should be made or not made, and how to make sure that the right action is taken to make the change happen successfully.

Fortunately, the best solution works for both challenges. First, make the strategy clear and easy to understand for everyone. This helps people to know how to contribute positively to the strategy. It also increases the chances that people will want to contribute. Second, include people in the creation of the strategy and in its operational elements. Take them through the logic behind the strategy and the available choices so that the strategy comes to life.

It's also hugely important that you listen to what is being said. Resistance to change can pinpoint weaknesses and gaps while there is still time to strengthen and fill. Strategic thinking is continuous and so this kind of information should refine and challenge your views.

Another challenge is to try to develop an organisation that is hungry for change. One that is stable enough to be productive and effective, but also able to be flexible and open – even hungry for change. If good change is welcome then it won't be ignored unless it's judged to be a problem. And if your change-loving people don't like a change, then you should pay attention.

Success

Typically, successful new strategy is the result of the response to a desire for change. This desire for change builds up over time along with dissatisfaction with the way things are. But it is balanced by the costs and effort of making those changes. Change will only happen when there is more desire for change than for stability.

Your task is to respond intelligently to real desire for change (and improvement) that already exists. Work with the forces for change so that it becomes organic rather than mechanical. In this way, you are working with the people rather than against them. The friction involved is reduced and the chances are higher as you will – at least – be attempting something that is desired and respected by people.

Carefully follow a process that translates the strategy into five to seven principles that clearly indicate the kind of behaviour that is needed to succeed. Communicate those simple principles (and the logic behind the strategy) over and over again. Listen actively to dissent, discontent and feedback – use it to improve the strategy and the actions that follow from it.

Strategists' measures of success

→ You have identified the changes that are necessary to your strategy working.

→ The company's people are involved in a dynamic strategy process.

→ Change fatigue is avoided by engaging people with only necessary change.

→ Change tools are used to understand the nature of human change.

→ The company becomes comfortable with questioning and implementing change.

Pitfalls

If change becomes commonplace it may also become boring. The essential part of each new set of changes may be lost amid the other competing changes that have not yet been completed. Changes may be contradictory so that one set is ignored. Or conflicting changes are made even though they counteract one another. You can think you are making changes when you are not. Or you can underestimate the effort involved in making changes inherent in your strategy.

Strategists' checklist

■ Consider the scale and nature of the changes that the new strategy will bring. What has to change? How big are the changes? Who will be affected? Who do you need to really make the strategy work?

■ Think about the role of external change agents to help people imagine the future changes and the organisational responses and design.

■ Try to create change that people believe in because they have been part of designing the original strategy and its implications.

- Use force field analysis to assess the forces for and against any particular change (see page 197).

- Use animation and orientation models to explore whether your strategy and the way it is communicated will engage people (see page 195).

- Use Kotter's eight phases to examine how you move from initial strategy to completed implementation – and then start again (see page 199)

Related ideas

Chris Argyris proposes the idea of defensive routines to explain why organisations don't change. Individuals in different groups conspire to avoid difficult changes without confronting them directly. Others don't point this out because no one wants their own sanctuaries of inertia to be identified.

This has similarities to the Garbage Can theory of decision making. Michael Cohen, James March and Johan Olsen observed that groups of people tend to make easy decisions even when those decisions don't solve valuable problems. They delay difficult decisions, even when the delay is damaging.

As Giovanni Gavetti argues, in a behavioural approach to strategy the most successful strategies become attractive because they are extremely difficult for most competitors. Often it is possible to copy what the winning competitors are doing. But losing competitors may fail to get their heads around the necessary strategic logic. Leaders reject what they don't 'get'. Try to avoid this mistake by looking at competitors' actions through their eyes. Imagine until you understand.

Understanding what can go wrong

There are lots of things that can go wrong with your strategy. You may have picked the wrong positioning, product or combination of cost, differentiation or focus. Just as often, the path from strategy as an idea doesn't succeed in becoming strategy as a reality.

Frequency: Understand once and then review.
Key participants: You and your team.
Strategy rating: ****

The most famous example of a company understanding what could go wrong with its strategy is Shell. They used the power of scenario thinking to prepare themselves for a range of possible futures which included an oil supply crisis. When this happened – in the 1970s – Shell were more prepared intellectually (and practically) to adapt.

More recently, scenario planning helped in the post-apartheid transition in South Africa. Four different scenarios, each with a memorable title, encouraged open thinking about strategic choices and consequences. In Singapore, the government uses a three-year cycle of scenarios to help it anticipate threats and opportunities, deepen conversation and improve thoughtful, strategic action.

Objective

Many strategies – particularly change strategies – fail to deliver what was promised. It is easy enough to produce strategy that is not fit for purpose. You can even pay millions for someone else to fill in the boxes and tables to save you making the effort. Your document can be glossy but still fail.

If the direction is unclear or poorly understood then it is less likely to lead to coherent action. There will be tasks completed and projects attempted but they will not support the success of the strategy. It is important that there is a clear logic and clear principles for action. These principles provide the guidance to people throughout the company concerning what actions and what style of actions the strategy requires.

The strategy depends on the commitment of people who have to make the strategy work. If they don't believe in it they won't act on it. If they are not inspired by it, they won't put their best efforts into filling out the details. No strategy is complete on paper, it requires the engaged creativity of employees, partners and customers to make it complete.

People can fight back against a new strategy not because they disagree with it for the company, but because they dislike the consequences for their job or department. They may use a variety of resistance techniques. They may just do their jobs and ignore the implications of the strategy. They may deliberately attempt to stop the strategy working by speaking or working against it.

Alternatively, people may love the strategy (which is right) but it still fails because the skills necessary to complete the strategy are missing. It doesn't matter how hard people work if they don't know how to do the work necessary to bring the strategy to life.

Similarly, people may love the strategy and have the skills to do the work but fail because of a lack of discipline. Strategy can fail because of inadequate or inappropriate processes. It could fail because of a lack of resources. A lack of understanding on the part of those who create and lead strategy is the usual cause of the gap between idea and reality.

Context

There is no guarantee that a particular strategic direction is right – or that it will bring the hoped-for results. That is why this book emphasises the importance of creative strategy and reacting along with planning. Yet if there is no action then the desired success is unlikely. And if action is continually disjointed and counterproductive then good strategy will not work.

It is worth taking a careful look at the different ways your strategy can go wrong. It's worth asking what happens if you have:

- misjudged the size of the market;
- underestimated the costs involved in the plan;
- overestimated the support of partners;
- misunderstood key success factors and knowledge.

It makes sense to build a regular review of assumptions and progress into the formal strategy process. It is also valuable to include it in a continual part of your strategic thinking. What do we do if the strategy is wrong? This is part of the performance review process but will also reflect different leadership styles related to strategy and implementation. Each has its own guiding questions:

How do I formulate perfect strategy?

You could decide that you always know best and that your strategy is a perfect plan for success. You may spend so long thinking about perfect strategy that you forget that it has to turn into reality. There are many cases where CEOs and the big strategy consultants have expensively created complex documents with no thought of implementation.

How do I implement my strategy?

You think that your strategy is pretty much perfect but you do remember the value of getting it done. In this case the importance is to ensure strict obedience to a detailed plan for action. Detailed action plans may emerge that are cascaded down through collections of meetings at each level of the hierarchy.

How do I get top managers committed?

You feel that strategy implementation benefits from top manager commitment and so you try to involve them from the time you have formulated the strategy. You give them time to comment and to give you feedback. You want insights and detail about *how* they are going to make strategy work rather than questions or contributions that change strategy.

How do I involve everyone in strategy?

You may choose to move between the strategy you have in mind and what you learn about the real-world implications of the strategy. You involve people throughout the organisation partly as a way of getting them involved but also because they have insights into the strategy direction *and* its implementation. Their insights may change intention, position and even create alternative strategies that replace the original strategy you had in mind.

Challenge

You want to test your strategy out, submit it to some criticism or at least some imagined scenarios. This doesn't have to be years or months of effort, just the focus of some experience mixed with creativity.

- What could go wrong with your strategy?
- What could go wrong in the external environment?
- How could the competitive assumptions be flawed?
- What could go wrong internally to stop implementation?

Use the various tools in the strategist's toolkit to examine the downside to the future. You can use the SWOT analysis to look specifically at the strengths, weaknesses, opportunities and threats to your strategy. You can apply scenario thinking to different future events and their impact on your strategy.

What could go wrong?	How could we respond?	How can we prepare?

What could go wrong?

It's worth starting with the problems that come to mind first. Strategic intuition can be very effective as an analytical shortcut. Put together a list of the things that could go wrong. Ask colleagues to do the same. Put them together to examine common concerns and minority insights. Use ideas throughout the book and particularly about risks on page 32.

How could we respond?

Think about responses to each of the key potential problems. What would you do in response to competitor threats? Or to suppliers or supply difficulties? Or if your product proved more or less popular than planned? How long would you wait before making changes to the strategy? What could you do to change operational plans and processes to support the strategy if things go wrong?

What can we do now to prepare?

Think about the kind of processes you can put in place to flag up problems with the strategy. Think about how to make sure you can rapidly change some aspects of the strategy. The strategy is not as important as the health and success of the organisation, so be prepared to sacrifice temporary pride to preserve longer-term reputation.

Success

Getting the strategy to work is ongoing, but recognising and preparing for what goes wrong is important to do on its own terms. You will value flexibility in the organisation more if it safeguards you and allows more risky, worthwhile or lucrative strategies to be pursued. Success is figuring out what the problems may be, what you will do to respond, and how you can prepare the organisation now. A sensational Plan B is a strategist's best friend.

Strategists' measures of success

➤ You have thought about different ways your strategy might fail.

➤ You have considered how leadership styles cope with strategy problems.

➤ There is a shared list of things that may go wrong.

➤ You have prepared for what can go wrong in the future.

➤ You have an organisation ready to adapt to future problems.

➤ Your strategy is adapted (where possible) to avoid problems.

Pitfalls

Thinking about what can go wrong can become an obsession. People can start to avoid doing anything that can go wrong. This kind of obsession is one of the things that can go wrong. You may become too cautious to make the strategy succeed. It's tempting to either avoid problems or to wait for problems. The better course is to keep people flexible so you can adjust and react.

Strategists' checklist

▪ Think about what can go wrong with your strategy. Include the possible problems in meetings because discussing the downside is an important part of how to make your strategy work.

▪ Creatively consider what you can do now about problems that may occur in the future. How would disaster change your strategy? What impact would changes in government have? What in the big picture could affect your strategy?

Related ideas

Larry Bossidy and Ram Charan argue – in the book *Execution* – that it is the discipline of getting things done that really separates success-ful and unsuccessful strategy. People, strategy and operations have to work together with dialogue, honesty and realism. Yet be warned: some organisations and leaders suffer from an execution obsession. Getting the wrong thing done well is still the wrong thing.

Saving your company from failure

Organisations fail. But they don't have to. Clever strategy can play a big part in preventing failure. It can also make a valuable contribution to turning the company around when it is in danger. And strategy can also make you smart enough to know that failure must be faced and overcome many times. Saving your company from failure is business as usual.

Frequency: Regularly.
Key participants: Top management teams first.
Strategy rating: ****

Ford was facing failure. Sales were down 25 per cent. It revealed the largest loss in corporate history. Debts were so huge that its credit ratings reached junk status. Profit margins per car were low and the company announced that it would not return to an overall profit for another five years.

The new CEO had successfully turned around Boeing but this would be a big test of what he had learned. In his first meeting he listened to presentations, then stood up and said 'Guys, did you realise we are losing money?' This open, direct question allowed everyone to get behind making the tough decisions they had put off for so long. They refused government help, reduced costs, built partnerships – for connectivity, embraced powerful new waves like car-sharing – sold non-core businesses. Within a year they had returned to $750 million profit. And they keep growing.

Objective

Among your many strategic objectives, not failing is important. Yet an organisation is continually faced by threats. Competitors create some of them by moving faster or provoking unwinnable price wars. New entrants and new substitutes also cause problems because you are organised to compete in traditional ways. Yet the biggest threats are always the organisation's performance and its ability to adapt to changes in the external environment.

The external environment can make it harder or easier to survive. It can move faster. It can be more chaotic. But the external environment doesn't get to determine whether you succeed or fail. It is the organisation that succeeds or fails at adapting to the demands of the external environment. And so it is here that the strategist will most profitably focus attention.

There are lots of options when trying to turn around a company. Sometimes the distinction is made between operating turnarounds – *doing things differently* – and strategic turnarounds – *doing different things*. In reality, the two are linked so closely that you will have to do both.

Context

There is always a failure line for any business (see figure below). Beyond this point, no recovery is possible. You may not know exactly where it is, but it is lurking somewhere below acceptable performance. There are danger signs, but they may either not be

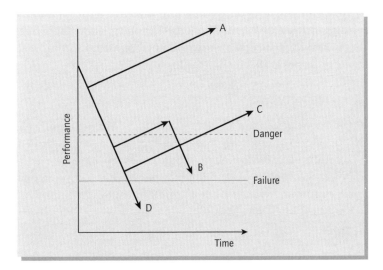

Recognising danger before failure

obvious because you don't know how to read them, or you may read them but not do anything about them. Stay away from the performance line of failure.

There are many reasons that nothing is done about danger signs. Your company may ignore them, claiming that the performance problem is just temporary. Your organisation may not know what to do about the problem even if it is recognised. It may not know why performance is getting worse. It may know why but not be able to figure out a solution or face making the tough decisions required by the necessary solutions.

Early, deep recovery

If you immediately recognise the problems, then find solutions and get them working, the turnaround can be very fast. And it can happen before you are even in the danger zone. You need to understand the causes of decline very quickly and be able to explain the necessary changes as desirable and urgent.

Shallow recovery

If you notice problems at some point and start work, that's good. If the company does only half a job, if you go with superficial change or delay important decisions, then the problems will come back. And they are often worse than before, with less time and fewer resources available than the first occasion.

Late, deep recovery

If you have noticed the problem for a while it requires a really big shock before the company makes the necessary decisions. And it takes really bad news before people are willing to make the necessary changes. This is costly but it may be the only way your company culture knows how to make significant improvements.

Challenge

Noticing the threat is the first part. You need to be aware of the performance in the organisation. And you need to be alert to changes outside of the organisation that may have an impact on business results. You can use the various tools in the strategist's toolkit to construct an early warning system.

- What threats could cause the failure of the company?
- How will you recognise the warning signs of failure in your business?
- Are there replacement products and new competitors?
- Have you been putting off important decisions?
- What are customers saying about your products and services?

If you can notice fast, then at least you have a chance of reacting fast. Some of this is about continual adjustment and can become part of business as usual. Improve the ability of the company to notice what is happening externally and internally so you don't sleepwalk into real problems.

Part of it is about learning to move really rapidly to cope with big shocks that threaten your business. In the Ford example, there was a mixture of long-term problems, the long emergency and sudden shocks related to the great recession. The strategist should be aware of all of these and help the company to deal with them all. Help your company to notice the expected and the unexpected. Explore with your colleagues how to notice each type of threat.

- Are you growing too fast? Are you getting sloppy with your expansion?
- Are your financial controls adequate?
- Is bureaucracy getting in the way of action?
- Which new competitors are more innovative? Or growing faster?
- How will social trends change demand for your products or services?
- What are your colleagues saying in employee surveys?
- Have you got the management skills necessary to be effective?

You need triggers to let you know when to respond. Some of these can be built into your management processes and control systems. Your balanced scorecard can help this to be about more than just financial indicators. Failure comes from not adapting, so internal company matters are as important as external ones.

Responding to the threat is the important next step. Denial can stop anyone doing anything because no one wants to be open about the problem. The first person to make a fuss about a potential threat may be ignored. They may even be criticised for being too pessimistic or difficult. If you notice the threat first you will have to consider how and when to get attention for the problem.

The cause of the threat is also related to how to respond. If you respond quickly and effectively to poor marketing then you can prevent the bigger problem of market share decline. If you delay responding to operational problems then they will escalate until they become strategic problems.

When a threat is noticed, managers tend to respond with the easiest, most obvious, least creative responses first. If that doesn't work then they will try something bigger although not necessarily more creative. They are likely to start with increasing control because control is what they understand. Next stop is reducing costs because that doesn't affect them directly.

Strangely, as the threats increase and performance decreases, the business will avoid doing anything directly to adapt to the threat or increase performance, even though that is exactly what they need. The best employees may leave the company because they can see what is coming. Others may remain, looking for excuses and scapegoats. Still nothing is done to respond creatively and directly to the problem.

It seems very difficult for top management to accept the loss of face involved in admitting that their direction and implementation are flawed. It is even more difficult for them to find alternatives to the way that they have always managed. They have given it their best shot and they have nothing else to give.

Sometimes good results save the company from making changes that would have brought about much better results. In this sense, good is the enemy of better but also the friend of eventual failure. There are many organisations that limp along strategically and operationally while churning out enough money to keep top management employed. In these cases, only sudden shocks externally and internally are enough to tip the balance towards action.

By the time a decision is eventually reached to make significant changes, there is often a new leader in charge. Sometimes existing leaders experience some kind of personal transformation that allows them to act like new leaders.

Success

The starting point for success is noticing the problem and looking at it clearly. There will need to be open and honest discussion about what is not working and what really has to happen. You need to distinguish between the old behaviours that got you into this mess and new behaviours that can save you.

It's important to deal with whatever (legal and ethical) action has to be taken to survive in the short term. These are usually financial issues. However, growth (and healthy business) does not come from cost cutting alone. You can cut your way to oblivion.

You will have a clear understanding of the problems. You will share this understanding with your colleagues. You will try to make this diagnosis as clear as possible. And you will set equally clear time limits and expectations on finding solutions and getting them started. Most failed turnaround efforts never really start, so cannot hope to finish.

If you are close to the failure line the most important thing is to focus. For instance, the standard advice is to resist the temptation to diversify. Such efforts can confuse the company at just the point that it needs clarity. This applies unless you have identified the end of the road for your particular market and you have enough cash to make the leap.

Getting better managers may be a solution; most companies who are successful have changed lots of the top team. But remember that the existing team may have solutions that they have not been empowered to try. So the more important step is to get those ideas out into the open and try them out.

Improving your managers by really getting them talking creatively and openly has huge benefits. It is powerful to bring in facilitation or coaching to give them the confidence, skills and strategic expertise necessary to save the company.

Reducing debt is not really a priority because the cash flow is an important way of surviving. The key is to find ways of being credible to creditors so that you can use your own cash to invest in solutions to your problems. You can reduce levels of debt later when it's in your financial interests.

Improving operational profit margins is useful because it allows you to make more money from your efforts to increase demand. And because it allows you to divert more funds into yet further improvements.

Improving marketing and innovation is essential. This doesn't just mean spending more on advertising – although it may. It means that marketing is everything between the customer who buys your products and the way you produce them. Understanding your customer better and creating smarter, more valuable products is the key to sustained success and turnaround.

Strategists' measures of success

- You know what could threaten the survival of your business.
- Everyone is looking for warning signs and discussing them openly.
- Potential delays to responding to threats are understood.
- Marketing and innovation are improved to keep the company adapting.
- You know the basic steps of avoiding failure and getting sustained growth.

Pitfalls

In times of crisis, it is natural to stop thinking clearly and keep going in the direction that is causing the problem. You may receive advice to adopt a top-down approach of issuing commands at a distance – this is wrong. You need to get a good feeling of the basics and to be prepared to make timely, clear decisions. But that isn't the same as being autocratic.

You also need to reach into the heart of the organisation for their diagnosis of what is not working. You need the engagement of your people and their experience. It is tempting to stop listening, or to be overwhelmed by the problems. It is important to focus clearly on improving the inside of your organisation to deal with the real desires of your customers.

Strategists' checklist

- Explore the threats that you are facing or may face. Examine their causes and your potential responses. Think about how you will recognise them. What are the warning signs? At what point should you be concerned?

- Discuss the generic responses to performance problems. What can you do now to prepare? What can you do now to avoid the problems in the future? How can you use potential threats to engage the organisation in improving what it does now?

- Consider how you can create a better, more sensitive early-warning system. Plug in and listen to customers and all employees. Use staff surveys, group discussions, informal chats and anonymous noticeboards. Anything to make sure you're not the last to know.

- Develop a continuous marketing and innovation function that is hungry for change at all levels and capable of seeing and doing more clearly than competitors.

Related ideas

Donald Hoffman argues that there are generic strategies for recovery. *Restructuring* – change top managers and culture. *Cost reduction* – reduce expenses. *Sell assets* – get rid of non-core assets. *Change marketing and products* – defensively and offensively seek to increase demand. *Repositioning* – find new markets and customers. These need to be creatively and decisively used together in ways that fit your circumstances and strategy.

The Strategy Book toolkit

Strategy is not the same thing as strategy tools or models. Yet it's useful to know what they are so you can deal effectively with corporate strategy. And if you use them *with* the principles and challenges in the rest of the book, they can be effective ways of organising and sharing your strategic thinking.

In this section, I have chosen a personalised selection of strategy tools. First, there are the most popular tools – those that are used most often in the workplace. Second, there are some of the most influential tools from the field of strategy and management. Third, there are tools that I have found valuable in my work with some of the most successful organisations in the world.

They are presented in an effective form so that they are straightforward to use. The idea is that you can really make a difference in offering better strategic thinking to your team, department or organisation.

Some well-known strategy tools have been omitted deliberately because they offer little in addition that is helpful. Where space allows these are referenced as similar to those that are included.

The basic (powerful) strategy questions

Strategists can get so interested in everything that they forget to make it clear what strategy is and – just as important – what questions strategy answers. There are some benefits from being mysterious but it's more powerful to make sure people know what strategy does. It's even more powerful if *you* use the questions to shape your own thinking.

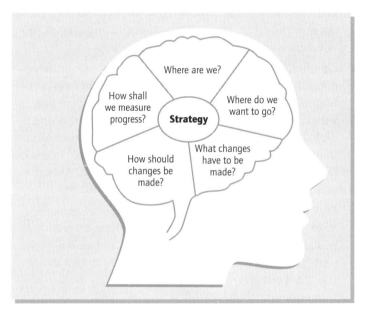

Shaping the future with fundamental questions

How to use

There are five basic questions that strategy tries to answer. Strategy is deliberately trying to shape the future by asking these questions.

Get the questions above clear in your head. Use these questions to organise the way you think about your organisation. A strategist should have an opinion about where the organisation is now (and where it's come from). You should be asking: Where do we want to go next? And keep these questions in mind when asking about the changes that need to be made, how they should be made and how you can measure progress.

The answers to the questions are all interrelated. And changes in any one answer will have an impact on the answers to all the others. The strategist's job is to have a grasp of the big picture – the answers to these questions.

- *Ask questions.* You don't have to be irritating but you can ask people for information about these questions and their answers. Find out where you think the business is. Look at industry magazines and websites. Search for your company name on the web. Talk to colleagues. Talk to customers. Figure out how you are 'positioned' in terms of pricing, quality and uniqueness in your location and your market.

- *Compare the organisation.* Get a feeling for how the business is doing. Look at the numbers, but also at the reputation of the business. Again use the web, magazines and conversations with customers and colleagues. But this time you're trying to really find out the way people think about you in the business that you are in. Are you best, second best, fifth best? Do people love you? Hate you? Do they want you to succeed? Are you growing or shrinking? Is the future bleak or brilliant?

- *Look forward and outwards. Think about where the organisation could go.* Use the various tools and strategy challenges in this book to provoke better strategic questions and more effective strategic thinking. Collect brands and examples that motivate you – that you love – and think about how they relate to what your business does.

- *Look inside.* How big does the organisation want to grow? What is the appetite for change? What kind of change does the organisation want to make? What are people talking about? Where are the (strategic) tensions? Where are the opportunities? What is moving faster than you?

These questions help you to be a better strategist. And if you get better at asking other people these questions then you will be valued as a more strategic thinker. Particularly if you have your own opinions and knowledge.

SWOT analysis

In the real world of business, SWOT analysis is the most popular of all the strategy tools. It's probably because it's easy to remember and seems logical (even obvious). It's a very practical, efficient way to start exploring the bigger picture and deciding what to do next.

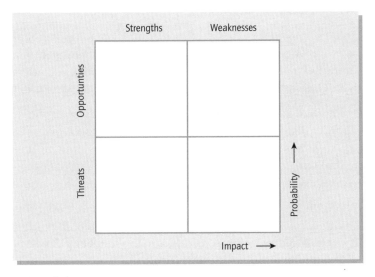

SWOT analysis

How to use

Draw up the grid. Then just list opportunities and threats facing you and the strengths and weakness of your organisation. Write up everyone's ideas. No need to be lengthy or provable at this point. The goal is to end up with a collective view of the most important issues under each heading.

■ Get everyone to think hard and imaginatively about the whole organisation and its external context (see page 134).

■ Consider the links between the four boxes. What strengths will allow you to take advantage of opportunities or overcome threats? What weaknesses need to be addressed to benefit from them?

■ Prioritise your lists by looking at their relative impact and probability.

■ Turn prioritised lists into specific strategies (or plans) with dates and owners. The SWOT analysis can move from thinking to action.

As an example, Uber use a mobile-based smartphone app to connect customers with available nearby taxis. Their strategy combines the strengths of the founders to directly target the weaknesses of traditional taxi firms.

The founders were both strong in their understanding of mobile software. They both had personal investment funds *and* networks in the heart of Silicon Valley to raise further funding and attention. These strengths created opportunities.

Traditional taxi firms were often slowed down by an unwieldy blend of disconnected organisation, with many smallish firms with a tactical perspective and dangerously low investment. They were also made vulnerable by complacent customer service expectations. These weaknesses invited threats.

When Uber launched, a new generation of customers loved how Google Maps showed how long they would have to wait, the ability to give feedback on taxi drivers, and the simplicity of paying automatically at the end of every journey.

Porter's 5 forces of competition

Your strategy has a competitive context. There are external forces – made up of the actions of buyers/customers, existing competitors, new entrants, new products and suppliers. This model helps you to see those forces more clearly and respond to them strategically.

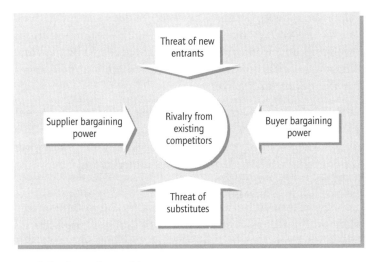

Porter's five forces of competition

Source: Adapted from Porter, M. E., 'How competitive forces shape strategy', *Harvard Business Review*, Harvard Business School Publishing, March/April 1979

How to use?

Put the diagram up for the group to see. Start by getting a general feel for whether (and by how much) the forces are increasing or decreasing. Use a corresponding number of plus or minus signs to illustrate. Try to illustrate the group's gut feeling with specific examples to bring each competitive force to life.

- Consider why a particular force is increasing and decreasing: Are barriers to entry coming down or up? Is your product easier or harder to copy or replace?

▪ Think about how you could change a force in your favour: Can you work more closely with partners or customers? Can you build on added value features and systems that reduce the threat of substitutes?

▪ Explore examples carefully: Do new entrants have a strategy that you can counteract? What happens if you stop competing with them? What would be the result if the forces continue to increase or decrease?

Take as an example *The New York Times*, founded along with thousands of other daily newspapers amid a mass communications revolution. In a world giddy on messages delivered by train and telegraph, they printed 'all the news fit to print' and became a mass money-making market leader.

In the USA, the immediate threat of new direct entrants is not great because the *NYT* won the traditional newspaper war in a market where readership and advertising is declining. The danger is from substitutes, the blogs, tweets, instagram and videos that provide news and opinion via the internet.

The *Huffington Post* started up amid similar competitive energy along with millions of other blogs with opinion-based articles labelled by some as amateur and shallow. The problem for the *NYT* is that ad space buyers liked the much lower prices and online readers quickly became used to not paying at all.

Despite a new logo that proclaims 'all the news fit to click', the *NYT* has found it hard to attract the very best suppliers of digital skills and twenty-first century internet journalism. Efforts to throw up paywalls have largely failed amid new forces of competition in a new market where the *NYT* 'journalism advantage is shrinking'.

Porter's generic strategies

Porter also argued that there are only three general strategies for achieving higher than average performance. You can be the cost leader through efficiency. You can develop unique products or services that are differentiated. Or you can focus on niche markets.

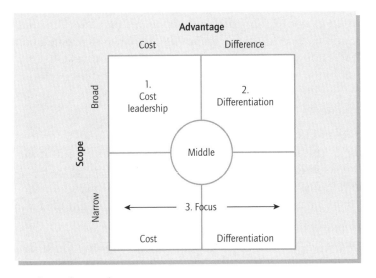

Porter's generic strategies

How to use

You can use the model to figure out how your current strategy fits within the extremes of cost leadership, differentiation and focus. Who is the cost leader in your market? Who has the most unique product or service? What narrow segments are being looked after by you and your competitors?

According to Porter, you have to choose between one of the three if you want above-average returns. He claims that being stuck in the middle is bad for business. But experience shows huge benefits to those who can accomplish low costs *and* differentiate their products. You can use this model to consider the benefits of reducing costs, differentiating your products or focusing.

Can you move from one advantage to another? The traditional route is from (1) low cost to (2) focused differentiation to (3) broader differentiation in the mass market. Each stage provides resources (and credibility) to grow and, done right, it can convince competitors to get out of your way and let you in.

As an example, consider Ryanair. It was just another small loss-making airline when its new CEO decided to pursue a cost leadership strategy influenced by the USA's Southwest Airlines. Part of the secret to his success was making this strategy clear to potential passengers *and* pursuing it relentlessly in day-to-day operations.

Ryanair has also marketed itself to a narrower group – a low-cost focus. This includes people who are willing to accept out-of-the-way European airports and a garish no-frills aesthetic. Traditionally, Ryanair do not offer business-class flights or airport lounges. They demand payment for seat reservations, inflight food and printing tickets. They use controversy to gain attention.

More recently, low-cost competitors have pressured Ryanair's plans for continued growth. Some offer lower prices. Some offer better service at the same prices. Others sell a little bit more for a slightly higher price. Ryanair has responded to competitor differentiation by offering a new business-class ticket and relaxing their more divisive policies. They are closer to the middle, but is it dangerous or smart?

Burgelman's strategy dynamics model

Creation of strategy does not happen in a vacuum. It happens in an environment that can be stable or dynamic. It's worth knowing what kind of industry you are facing. And it's also valuable to know what kind of organisation you are dealing with.

	Company	
	Rule-abiding	Rule-changing
Environment — Rule-abiding	Limited industry change	Controlled industry change
Environment — Rule-changing	Independent industry change	Runaway industry change

Burgelman's strategy dynamics model
Source: Adapted from Robert A. Burgelman

How to use

This model is useful in reviewing the kind of dynamic that any strategy you create will have to work with. It has two key components: the level of change in the industry (or the environment of the industry), and the amount of change made by individual companies, including yours. Consider:

- *Levels of rule changes in your environment.* Is the industry fairly stable with relatively predictable changes made in accordance with well-established rules? Is competition limited to features and criteria that are well understood? Are there changes in the environment that are beyond the actions of individual companies? Are there changes in the structure of the industry? How about the legal basis for the industry? Or its technological basis? Or new entrants or substitute products?

▪ *Levels of rule changes by individual companies.* Are there companies that are changing the rules of competition? Is anyone trying out new business models? Are individual companies challenging the contradictions and constraints of the industry? How many individual companies are challenging (or changing) the rules? Is your company one of the rule-changers?

Back in the late 1970s, Vincent McMahon's WWE was a rule-changer in the rule-abiding industry of professional wrestling. At first, this allowed the company to benefit from controlled industry change. They went outside traditional geographic boundaries to create entertainment with national TV syndication and global appeal.

WWE started to face independent industry change outside of their control. New internet-based entertainment offered new formats and a free-to-view business model from alternatives like the Ultimate Fighting Championship. And because WWE continues to break the rules, the context for their success is runaway industry change.

Porter's value chain and value system

The ability of your company to compete successfully is about everything the company does and how everything is organised. The value chain is a useful way of looking at the whole organisation while the value system helps you to look at how you fit into a bigger picture.

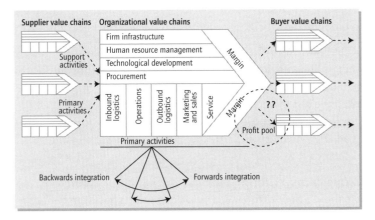

Porter's value chain

How to use

Think of your company as a chain of activities within a wider value system that leads to overall results. Divide what your company does into *primary* activities that directly produce and deliver products and *support* activities that make primary activities possible. Then start asking questions.

- How well do the individual functions perform?
- What could you do to improve how different functions fit together to provide competitive advantage? Which steps and parts can be added or removed?

- Do individual functions measure up to the best in the world? Does the overall value system magnify advantages?
- How do you compare to your competitors' value chains and systems? Where are the profit pools in your market?

Explore your value chain and system for how effectively they add value to the customer. You also want to know how well they contribute to your strategic performance. Look for opportunities – and threats – from strengths and weaknesses in the overall system.

Hermès is a multi-million-dollar luxury fashion brand founded as a nineteenth-century Parisian workshop making harnesses for the aristocracy. The sons of the founder grew their team of craftsmen to produce an expanding range of accessories, clothing, handbags and scarves.

They sold goods via retail partners and their own forward-integrated shops. They also expanded via partnership, relying on the expertise of a Swiss watch manufacturer. Hermès introduced the iconic Duc carriage logo in the 1950s. They successfully strengthened their primary activities by hiring top designers and retail expertise.

Hermès increased forwards integration by reducing franchises and expanding their own company-owned shops. Backwards integration also increased as they bought crocodile farms and tanneries. They nurtured their advantage in what Hermès call metamorphosis – their ability to make precious materials even more precious through the work of skilled craftsmanship. They deepen their profit pools.

Core competencies and resource-based view

As a strategist, you need to look at what resources you have at your disposal. You need to understand how the collection of skills, knowledge, tangible and intangible property can provide strategic capabilities. And you need to see creatively how these competencies create opportunities or can be used to pursue opportunities.

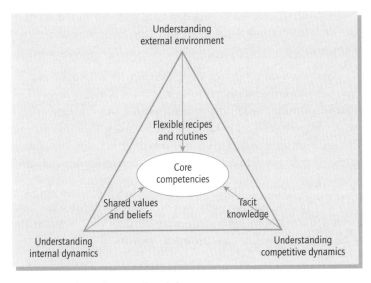

Core competencies and resource-based view

How to use

Core competencies are a combination of resources and capabilities available to an organisation. They are sometimes referred to as strategic assets when they offer a distinctive capability, particularly when that capability is viewed as helpful in achieving the organisation's objectives.

Seek to understand the key components of your external environment (politics, social, technological and more). Look at the competitive dynamics in your market or strategic group and the internal dynamics of your organisation.

Explore what makes your company distinct. What are your shared values and beliefs? What kinds of embedded tacit knowledge or deep smarts do you have? What are the recipes and routines?

The idea is to find valuable recipes and rare ingredients that others don't have, that are difficult to imitate, and then organise to turn them into survival and sustainable competitive advantage.

As an example, consider Flight Centre. Its founder, veterinarian 'Scroo' Turner, started selling discount airfares on the Australian high street some thirty years ago. His unconventional recipe worked.

Officially, everyone joins the Flight Centre tribe with shared values and beliefs from profit incentives that invite a sense of ownership. Flexible routines benefit from seven-person teams – or families – who compete with other families and villages. Tacit knowledge, the kind not written down, is based on employee expertise and experience with travel to deliver superior customer service and sales.

When the founder stepped down as CEO, a huge profits dip earned the company the nickname of 'Flightless Centre'. The CEO returned – along with his customary declarations of 'What the f*ck is going on here?' – *and* profitable growth.

What if the CEO fails to understand the external environment by wrongly ignoring government pressure? Or misunderstands the competitive dynamics of the internet? Or misses key internal dynamics that are over dependent on him for independent thinking?

The danger is that Flight Centre gets its core competencies wrong. It may value being seen as one of the best companies to work with while simultaneously delivering poor customer service. Or fail to grow because it doesn't grasp the DIY ethic of direct booking or the heightened aesthetic of new services like Airbnb or Hipmunk.

Nonaka and Takeuchi's knowledge spiral

You want to figure out what you are best at so you can turn it into a strategic advantage. Part of what you might be best at is how you learn and what you know. These abilities can become strategic assets. They can provide the basis for differentiating strategy.

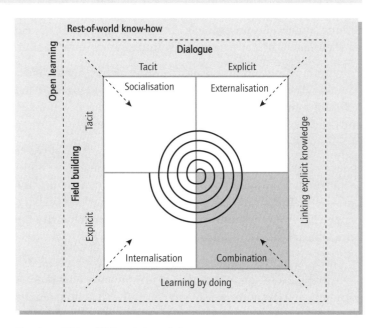

Nonaka and Takeuchi's knowledge spiral

Source: Adapted from Nonaka, I. and Takeuchi, H., *The Knowledge-Creating Company*, Oxford University Press, 1995

How to use

There are different kinds of knowledge and learning. *Tacit* is what we know without writing it down or clearly stating it. *Explicit* is what we know that has been written down or clearly stated. The idea is you should understand how knowledge is created and ways of sharing that knowledge.

Socialisation is where most new knowledge comes from. People learn from and share experiences. They talk, observe, imitate, brainstorm and just kind of 'pick up' skills that shape what they do and think. *Internalisation* tries to formally teach knowledge that is written down already – this is traditional training. *Externalisation* tries to write down your own *secret recipes* using models and checklists so that they are simpler to learn. *Combination* puts secret recipes and formal knowledge together to create better ways of doing what you want to accomplish.

Identify how you learn. Find your secret recipes and combine them with the best formal knowledge. Warning: It's not about traditional knowledge management. The knowledge spiral can help you become the best at learning and using what you have learned.

The Toyota Way helped it become the world's largest vehicle manufacturer. The company gained valuable tacit knowledge through learning by doing. This learning was gained by generations of engineers – known as gods – getting their hands dirty.

Unfortunately, explicit knowledge can become inflexible rules that can threaten the survival of those who unthinkingly follow them. This is why Toyota is replacing robots with humans because humans can learn. And this is why Daihatsu, a Toyota subsidiary, jumped back into the knowledge spiral. They wanted to halve the price of their mini-car so it could win in emerging markets.

Engineers, sent to the procurement department by the Daihatsu CEO, found over-expensive parts and an over-cosy sales process with long lunches and excessive stability. The CEO declared the new explicit rule was to find lower-cost parts from any supplier, anywhere in the world. This included learning from generic – or fake – manufacturers in China and India. New lessons for a new world.

Peters, Athos and Waterman's 7-S framework

Strategy depends on combining lots of parts in a way that can deliver. Even if your strategic position and intentions are good, you still need to remember the importance of fitting parts together. This model was designed to consider connections between each of those parts – and to remind you that 'structure is not organisation'.

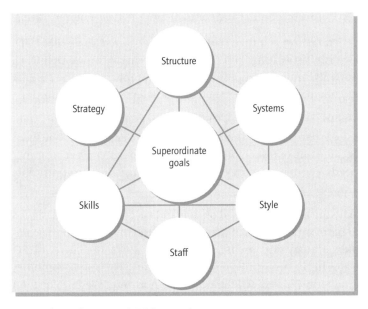

Peters, Athos and Waterman's 7-S framework

How to use

The 7-S model was created to show that strategy is about more than managing a portfolio of businesses (corporate strategy). And that organisation is more than structure. Each element of each business has to be organised in a way that creates success. This combination of parts can support the formal strategy or change the strategy thanks to effective, creative management.

One way to use the 7-S model is to figure out how to make the parts work together in a *coherent* way. How can each part be aligned to the others? What is the best way for each part to be operated? What skills, systems, style, staff and structure are necessary to the strategy? Are the overall (or superordinate) goals achieved by the combination of parts? How do shared values shape actions?

Another way to use the 7-S model is to look for tensions between these as a source of opportunity. What can you learn from contradictions and conflict? What opportunities will allow revolutionary change? How can you keep on the edge of strategic innovation? How can you keep renewing the strategy? How can you transcend conflict and contradictions to create new markets?

When Lenovo acquired IBM, they also acquired an ex-IBM CEO. He didn't stay long. Nor did his replacement, an ex-Dell CEO. Both attempted to impose values and approaches to the 7Ss that did not make the most of their diverse talents and opportunities.

The founder returned as CEO. Together with his staff he established shared values, the 5Ps, to guide the Lenovo Way. The focus became one of leveraging diversity to help better meet customer needs – something they view as a key ingredient to profitable growth.

Skills are rebalanced based on demand via cross-training designed to harness the talents of their staff. Instead of relying on the complex strategy documents of his predecessors, the current CEO states his in two words: protect and attack. Their style combines long-term Chinese-style strategy and short-term Western focus on earnings.

Scenario planning

You're trying to shape the future, but the future is uncertain.
Scenarios can help people to anticipate, make sense of, and learn
about the future. By accepting uncertainty, you can become better
at developing strategy and making it work.

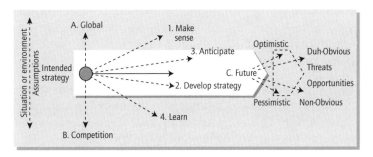

Scenario planning

How to use

List assumptions you're making about the future (C) for your intended strategy to work. Consider what has to happen inside and outside your company to be successful. Identify the most uncertain and
the most impactful assumptions. Then start playing imaginatively
with trends and traditions to explore new, non-obvious futures.

All scenario planning should bring assumptions into the open
(transparency) and increase the range of options considered (diversity). Focus moves from what is happening globally (A) and
what competitors are doing (B) to considering a range of obvious
and less obvious scenarios for the future (C).

- *Making sense*: How does a complex problem or area of
  uncertainty work in practice? What does a trend mean?
- *Anticipate changes*: What might happen in the future? What
  might competitors (B) do? What could lead to opportunities
  or threats? What is happening globally (A)?

- *Learning*: What can be learned about what is happening? About the nature of customers? Or competition? Or how you think? How can you learn more by experimenting?
- *Develop strategy*: How flexible is your strategy? What other options are there? Can you find better ways of shaping the uncertain future?

Marvel Comics entered bankruptcy back in the 1990s because its main owner used its success to finance failed investments. It escaped bankruptcy with the help of a kind of strategic scenario thinking. The new CEO and leadership had experience of turnarounds that helped make sense and anticipate the challenges faced in the short-term and long-term future.

They developed strategy to gain multiple benefits based on flexible future scenarios and hypotheses. They moved to a licensing model for new markets, including TV, clothing, video games and movies. Short term, Marvel increased cash, boosted its worldwide brand and reduced debt. Medium term, they learned how to win in new markets and avoid others – like the internet. Longer term, they used funds *and* expertise to invest in their own self-developed blockbuster games and movies.

They rediscovered the value in the Marvel comic book universe and adapted it into the Marvel cinematic universe. They hired lifelong comic book fans as key executives, producers, screenwriters and actors. They moved in directions non-obvious to competing movie studios and comic publishers – and, with imagination, shaped a future so attractive that Disney snapped them up in a multi-billion-dollar deal.

Ansoff's growth grid

Most businesses want to grow. It's difficult to decide when to launch new products and when to get into new markets. The growth grid can make choices clearer. Groups of people can also get involved in the discussion. It can also help you make decisions about strategy.

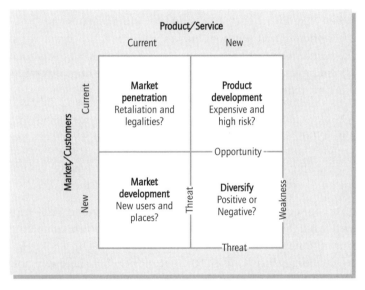

Ansoff's growth matrix

Source: Adapted from Ansoff, I., 'Strategies of diversification', *Harvard Business Review* 25(5), Harvard Business School Publishing, 1957

How to use

Start by listing current markets, products and services. Examine threats, opportunities, strengths and weaknesses (SWOT analysis). Think about the existing and new market and products (5 forces). Figure out what unique capabilities you offer (value chain).

■ What are the opportunities and threats in new markets and in new products? Would it be easier (or more rewarding) to move into a new market? Is the risk of launching new products too high?

- Have any of your competitors launched new products? Are any competitors from markets where you do not compete? Do your capabilities give you a competitive advantage?

It's valuable to use the growth grid to keep discussions going about choices. Situations will change over time and the grid can help you remember the logic (and assumptions) of decisions made in the past and when to change them. Try to select new markets for positive rather than negative reasons – find advantages that help you win.

When Nike launched its Fuelband to existing markets and customers, the product was new, and ahead of its main competitors. Product development was expensive and high risk but the launch was successful – leading to a significant increase in profits for its equipment division.

Two years later, Nike changed its approach because of maturity and competition in a crowded market. The Fuelband hardware was popular, but software and partnerships are seen as the best way of winning big. They can diversify in a manner that achieves economies of scope around core capabilities and management skills.

Nike connected with 18 million users via their online Nike+ ecosystem but they want the hundreds of millions who use competing smartphone apps and trackers. They have opened up a Nike+ lab to collaborate since there is little strategic benefit to hardware now the fitness tracker market has developed. Nike growth strategy is dynamic. It plays to win, adapting to strengths and opportunities.

The Boston Consulting Group (BCG) growth share matrix

It can be difficult to prioritise focus on specific markets and products. The product portfolio matrix organises products by market growth and market share. You can then target investment in products that best support the strategy and objectives of the organisation. Use with creativity and caution, as it is often more dangerous than helpful.

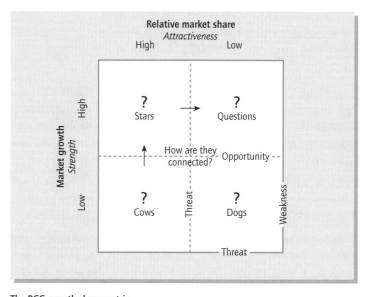

The BCG growth share matrix

Source: Adapted from The BCG Portfolio Matrix from the Product Portfolio Matrix, © 1970, The Boston Consulting Group (BCG)

How to use

The idea is to find market growth and share for the products (or divisions or subsidiaries) you are focused on. A relative estimate is enough at the early stage. The objective is to organise what you have into four groups so that you can decide how best to prioritise effort and investment. It is a tool for thinking.

Should you invest more in stars but less in cash cows because they can't grow? Or invest in cash cows to protect revenues? Will rethinking dogs transform their fortunes? Or have they really no future at all? Can question marks be made into stars? All of this can be misleading – or enlightening - depending on how it is done.

Warning! There are major pitfalls with unthinking use of this matrix. Markets are not generally clearly defined. Market share is not the same as profitability (or desirability). And specific opportunities and threats may completely change investment criteria. Better to take a balanced strategic view than be blinded by the labels.

When the BCG matrix was created, relative market share was assumed to be linked with profitability. Its creators argued firms with higher market share than nearest rivals would have more know-how. Firms with greater know-how could enjoy lower costs and higher profits compared to their nearest rivals.

Other matrices are available. McKinsey and GES matrix has nine cells organised by business unit strength and industry attractiveness. The BCG Advantage Matrix compares number of competitive advantages with size of advantages. There's even a two-by-two matrix for social entrepreneurs, by Robert Gruber and Mary Mohr. You can choose 'necessary evils' with high returns and low social benefit or push for 'best of all possible worlds' with high returns and social benefits.

Simplistic use of strategic tools can lead to stupid strategy. The creator of the BCG matrix was aware of the pitfalls, but those using such models may not be. Managing a mixed portfolio may be a good idea, but craft ways to group your effort that work for you. And look for the best opportunities to nurture ideas, products and companies.

Corporate raiders and private equity firms gained poor reputations and rich lifestyles by finding companies with low valuations relative to potential. Marvel, discussed earlier, was bought by a raider who 'milked the cow'. Only after bankruptcy did a turnaround investor transform dogs, cows, and question marks into stars with a connected strategy. With real stakeholder value.

Kim and Mauborgne's four actions

It can be easy to get trapped in doing the same things for the same customers. There are business habits that become fixed in particular companies or industries. The blue ocean approach asks whether it's possible to change the value curve and focus on non-customers.

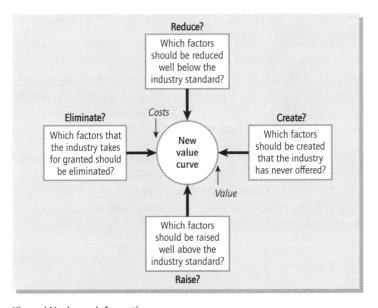

Kim and Mauborgne's four actions

Source: Adapted from Kim, W. C. and Mauborgne, R., *Blue Ocean Strategy: How to create an uncontested market space and make the competition irrelevant*, Harvard Business School Publishing, 2005

How to use

Look at your product in the light of customer *and* non-customer preferences. Think about how the product is used and how it compares to the industry average (or rules) for products. Then imaginatively consider whether non-customers would buy if you changed some of the industry assumptions.

You could *reduce* some attribute, *eliminate* it completely or *raise* the level or quality of the attribute. You could also *create* some feature that has never been seen in your particular industry (or market) before. You want to increase value while decreasing the cost of providing what your target customers don't appreciate.

In a sense, this is an approach to differentiating your product from others (see page 62), entering new markets (see page 93) or disrupting through innovation (see *The Innovation Book*). It has received criticism for impracticality yet is useful in generating ideas to creatively redesign core competencies or the value chain.

You are trying to avoid *red oceans* where everyone is doing the same thing for the same customers and instead minimise competition by finding strategic gaps in new market spaces – *blue oceans*. This kind of value innovation has been used to explain the success of Cirque du Soleil, who created a new market space, and Dyson, who were quickly attacked by aggressive competitors.

Often this is a reaction to opportunity rather than a deliberate attempt to find unchallenged market space. Pandora, for example, started selling charm bracelets. These became a Lego-like system of bracelets and rings attractive to non-traditional customers. A luxury product in affordable parts – accessible to friends and family.

Greiner's growth (and crisis) model

Strategy may consider the internal challenges you face. These challenges change throughout the history (and growth) of the organisation. The *growth model* suggests different challenges for different phases. It describes each of these challenges as a crisis.

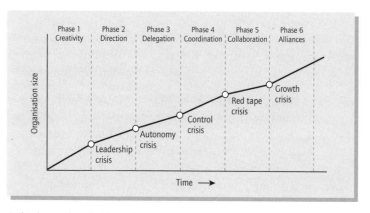

Greiner's growth and crisis model

Source: Adapted from Greiner, L. A., *Evolution and Revolution as Organizations Grow*, Harvard Business School Publishing, 1998

How to use

Consider the history and current status of your organisation. Think about what kind of phases and crises have been experienced since it was started. It's particularly valuable as a framework for discussion. It can provide a structure for a group to better understand the challenges and solutions required from strategy.

An organisation starts with *creativity* until it reaches a leadership crisis with people looking for *direction*. Eventually leadership is overwhelmed, leading to an autonomy crisis with people needing *delegation*. In turn, autonomy can cause a control crisis that requires additional *coordination*. The instinct for control risks a red tape crisis that needs a more fluid *collaboration*. And, finally, a growth crisis is reached that prompts a search for external *alliances*.

This model isn't a perfect predictor of what happens in each organisation. The phases may be skipped or repeated. The benefit of the model is to consider whether *something like* the crises described here is a good fit for your challenges. It then helps you consider the kind of solutions naturally needed.

In a sense, this is about strategically refining the available means to make it more likely that you will achieve desirable ends. When Twitter, discussed earlier in this book, reached its seventh anniversary it had also reached a kind of leadership crisis.

The company's third CEO seemed to have the right background, with Andersen Consulting, and as a serial entrepreneur, to be a professional leader. And yet he had never led anything this big.

Ahead of listing publicly on the New York Stock Exchange, the company underwent yet another reorganisation. The CEO reduced the number of people directly reporting to him – down to only four. The idea was to make better use of their engineering brainpower. They wanted faster product improvements to a more focused strategy. Something that investors would be sure to demand.

A year later, the CEO had not yet found a stable organisation or a clearly defined strategy. People can't contribute effectively if everyone is building towards a different, ever-changing, target. To evolve as a company, Twitter needs to get past its current crisis and find sustained direction. One evolution and revolution at a time.

De Wit and Meyer's strategy tensions

There are always contradictions. There are always tensions in the way people look at things – and what they think should happen. Smart strategists learn to accept that there is not always one best way of organising means – or necessarily a single desirable end.

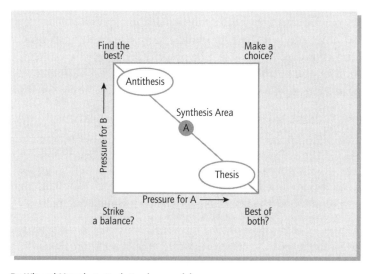

De Wit and Meyer's strategic tensions model

Source: Adapted from De Wit, B., Meyer, R and Heufens, P., *Strategy: Process, Content, Context: An International Perspective,* Cengage Learning, Inc., 2010

How to use

The model argues that strategy involves choices, and that those choices are guided by differing points of view. Every choice, or perspective, has an opposite. Every thesis has its antithesis. You can try to find the best solution, combine the best, make a choice or strike a balance between two extremes.

For any particular solution, it is worth considering the extreme opposites. If someone proposes revolution, consider evolution.

If the plan is for cooperation, ponder the benefits of competition. Where globalisation has become obvious, contrast it against localisation.

The aim is not to be awkward but instead to first look at the other side and then create clear alternatives without getting stuck in an eternal search for a perfect answer. As a result, you are more likely both to find clever combinations of the extremes that offer significant benefits and understand better the assumptions underpinning any particular argument.

One of the world's fastest growing retailers, Tiger, has succeeded by playing creatively with strategic tensions. Its Danish founders, Suzanne and Lennart Lajboschitz, wanted everything as simple and affordable as possible. The pressure for simplicity was about making the business easier to run, the pressure for affordability was about appealing to the broadest possible range of customers.

Yet, they also felt pressure to only sell things that were worth buying. They had a heart-felt desire to live what they describe as the 'give people more, charge them less' paradox. They do not see a low price as an excuse for delivering crappy products. Instead they took it as an opportunity to design their own high function, high emotion products, rather than relying on low-quality suppliers.

Described as the IKEA of the high street, or a dollar store of design, Tiger has more than 450 stores worldwide. It sells items including whimsical knitted teapot warmers, delightful snail-shaped tape dispensers, footballs and rubber ducks, all alongside quality basics.

Tiger could have tried to *make a choice* between low cost and high value – and ended up like any other pound or dollar discounter. They might have attempted to *strike a balance* between the extremes – much like a traditional big box retailer leaving the choice to customers. Instead they strive to find inspiration in synthesis – bring the very best of all worlds. There can be genius in synthesis.

Cummings and Wilson: orientation and animation

An important benefit of strategy can be helping to focus and motivate people's individual efforts. This model examines how much strategy *orients* the thinking and actions of an organisation. It also explores how well it *animates* and engages people.

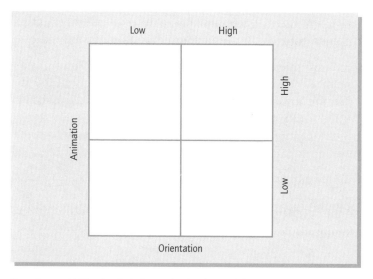

Cummings and Wilson's orientation and animation model
Source: Adapted from Cummings, S. and Wilson, D., *Images of Strategy*, Wiley-Blackwell, 2003

How to use

Consider to what extent people in the current organisation are animated (or motivated). Is morale high? Are people working hard and creatively? Then consider how effectively the current strategy helps orient the type of effort needed. Mark the current levels of both.

The next step is to think about how new strategy can improve levels of animation and orientation. How credible and novel is the new strategy? Will it be believed? Will it be understood?

How interesting is the strategy? What does it offer to the people whom you need to support the strategy?

It's also valuable to consider *how* the strategy is communicated and created. How many people are involved in its creation? What kind of activities and meetings involve them? Will your strategy help animate and orient partners and customers? Will people know what you are trying to do? Will they care?

Over at IKEA, they take great care to both animate (motivate) and orient (focus) effort from people who work for them. Part of this is their blend of training, coaching and self-managed learning. And part is how the style and substance of the employee experience is designed to match the overall strategic values and goals.

One recruitment campaign called 'Assemble Your Future' came complete with an IKEA-style instruction booklet for careers. Another job advert, in their corporate blue and yellow, asked for 'WHY-SAYERS' to join them – people who 'want to make things better. More fun. More clever.' They tend to pay more, to get much more.

IKEA wants practically minded people because it sells a practically minded product. Adventurers are wanted because IKEA depends on the development of its people's creativity. They want the best of the available talent and they want to put it to work strategically.

Lewin's force field analysis

The parent of modern change models is psychologist Kurt Lewin's force field analysis. It examines forces that restrain desired change and forces that drive desired change. It argues that restraining forces should be reduced so that desirable change can happen naturally.

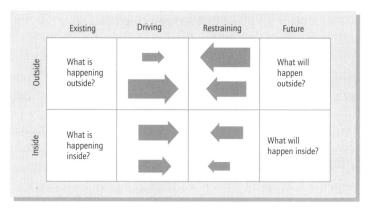

Lewin's force field analysis

How to use

In our improved version of the model, start by describing the kind of future situation that your strategy will create, on the outside and inside of the organisation. Then describe the existing situation in the same areas inside and outside the organisation.

Identify the reasons *driving* your strategic vision inside and outside the organisation. Are customers demanding the changes? Are competitors forcing improvements? Are employees suggesting things be done? Or is there government legislation?

List the *restraining* forces that might *halt* your desired strategic vision inside and outside the organisation. Are employees unhappy with changes? Do you have the right skills? Is your brand poorly positioned to make the changes?

Finally, examine how you can reduce the restraining forces, so that change happens naturally and with a minimum of conflict and wasted effort. But be careful not to discount so-called resistance since people often resist change for very good reasons – and these must be understood to improve your strategy.

In the confectionery business, there are many forces driving the industry towards change. There is pressure outside from campaigners who want fair trade because they feel it is ethically right and because it is a way of helping people escape poverty.

Green & Black is a brand that was developed because of the ethical beliefs of its founders. Retailers made shelf space for fair-trade products because of the driving force of customer demand – and despite the resisting forces of established confectionery giants.

Much later, Nestlé started to move very slowly towards fair trade and for quite different reasons. The main driving force did not appear to be ethical. The driving force was fear of losing sustainable supplies of cocoa because poor farmers were abandoning their farms. Nestlé have committed to supply chain transparency, invested in schools for farmers' children and given away new variants of cocoa plants. Because they fear a future without cocoa.

Kotter's eight phases of chang

Most strategy involves change in search of more success. It follows that the ability to make changes to organisations is of strategic importance. It is pointless creating a wonderful strategy if the strategy cannot be put into action. This is one approach to making changes.

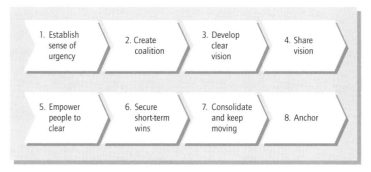

Kotter's eight phases of change

Source: Adapted from Kotter, J. P., *A Force for Change: How Leadership Differs From Management*, The Free Press, 1990. Reprinted with permission of The Free Press, a Division of Simon & Schuster, Inc. Copyright © 1990 by Kotter, J.P. All rights reserved. With additional rights courtesy of Kotter Associates, Inc.

How to use

There are many change models that follow more or less the same steps. They start with trying to do something to unfreeze the status quo and end by freezing the organisation so that it follows the new desired pattern.

In Kotter's model, there are eight steps. You start by establishing a sense of urgency based on potential crises and opportunities and then create a coalition with the credibility to lead change efforts. A clear vision is developed and then shared with people who are empowered to clear any obstacles in their way.

To build further belief in the strategic vision, highly visible short-term wins are sought. Further changes are made and consolidated in order to keep momentum building. At some point, particular changes are anchored to prevent them regressing back to the way that they were.

In practice, many different strategic projects and changes may overlap. This creates some difficult with knowing *when* to establish a sense of urgency and when to anchor change. It also leads to the problem of change fatigue where people simply cannot muster further enthusiasm for yet more change.

The newly appointed CEO of Mattel, the American toy maker, announced the company needed just such a 'sense of urgency' to produce new toys and become popular with younger customers. The previous CEO lost his job after Mattel lost its position as the No. 1 toy maker in the world. Hence the urgency.

The previous CEO shared a vision of 'creating the future of play' but the strategies that emerged were not successful. Meanwhile Lego became No. 1 and Hasbro shifted slickly from a focus on toys for boys to toys with universal appeal. Mattel was left behind.

Following fifty years of success with Barbie, Mattel have made many changes, but those changes have not been strategic successes. They failed with game consoles in the 1980s. And the $3.6 billion acquisition of the Learning Company in 1999 failed within a year.

This points to some of the strategic limitations of change models. Urgency does not guarantee success. Shared vision does not guarantee success. And quick wins can be big mistakes that, if anchored into business-as-usual, commit a company to failure.

Kaplan and Norton's balanced scorecard

Once you have a strategy in place, you will want to know how well it is doing. You don't want to just measure financial performance. The financial implications of a strategy are usually not immediate. There are lots of areas that contribute to the success of a strategy.

Kaplan and Norton's balanced scorecard

Source: Adapted from Kaplan, R. S. and Norton, D. P., 'The balanced scorecard: measures that divide performance', *Harvard Business Review*, Harvard Business School Publishing, 2005

How to use

You will never create the perfect balanced scorecard for your organisation. But you can move strategic focus to a range of measures that better reflect performance and progress towards your strategy.

First, include your vision and strategy. It doesn't have to be final but it helps to have a sense of what will be measured. Next, consider the business from four perspectives: financial, customer, processes and learning. What has to happen in all areas if your organisation is to be successful? How can you measure how well you are doing?

Don't get obsessed with the measures or the scorecard. Don't waste excessive amounts of time measuring. It may be enough to have a rough, opinion-based measure in many areas. The value here is in making the strategy come to life and giving people a more balanced view of what is important in what they do and achieve.

The CEO of Britvic, UK-based drinks producer and PepsiCo distributor, adopted the balanced scorecard, because of inconsistent financial performance.

He made the decision after a coaching workshop with 450 senior managers reviewed survey and performance data. The employee survey suggested that leadership was poorly regarded, while missed targets indicated a lack of accountability.

Leadership ratings *did* increase slightly but growth did not. More processes didn't help company creativity, stop a choking hazard product recall or save the job of the CEO or chairman when a competitor, AG Barr, attempted a takeover.

It was only when the chairman was fired that he had the time and space to gain a more strategic view. He was able to see the attractiveness of investing in dormant brands and global marketing for global growth. And when rehired, this time as a CEO, he immediately adopted a 'growth strategy' that has so far worked well – particularly with the launch of Fruit Shoot in India and the USA.

The smart strategist remembers that a balanced view is no substitute for a strategic view of strengths and weaknesses. The secret is to look for connections between the various measures that provide insights into threats – and seek attractive opportunities.

Hrebiniak's model of strategy execution

In recent years, there has been increasing focus on the execution of strategy. The idea is that having a wonderful strategy is not very useful if you can't make it work in the real world. Part of this is deciding to do the right thing, but the rest is getting the right thing done.

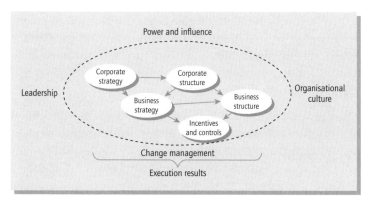

Hrebiniak's model of strategy execution

Source: Adapted from Hrebiniak, L. G., *Making Strategy Work*, Wharton School Publishing, 2005

How to use

The strategy execution model gives you a logical view of different parts of the organisation that will need decisions and action. Use it to think and discuss how all the parts fit together. Is this working well? Can it be improved?

Corporate strategy is about managing the business portfolio, the resources they get and what is expected. *Corporate structure* is about how much to diversify or focus, about whether to grow organically or through joining with other companies, and about how much to centralise or decentralise.

Business strategy is about individual business decisions about what products and services to offer, how to compete and how to be different. *Business structure* is about deciding how to organise, different kinds of hierarchy, or no hierarchy, geographical locations and functional groupings.

Each of these parts interacts with the others, and with effective choices for incentives and controls. This is about how to know what is going on, how to organise effort within the overall structure and get feedback on performance, and the kind of leadership style and cultural climate best for making your strategy happen. Incentives should encourage the kind of work you need.

When P&G bought Gillette, already a hugely successful company, they wanted to avoid failure. Part of this was making sure that the corporate level had something to offer to make them useful to their new business colleagues. How could they help Gillette win bigger?

From before the deal was done, corporate people moved beyond the basics of corporate structure and systems. They researched opportunities for growth with Gillette. They worked on plans for winning in new markets that combined expertise.

As a smart strategist, take advantage of working at a distance from the front line. Look for bigger trends, or waves of change. Identify patterns of strengths, weaknesses, threats and opportunity that the business-level people are too close to see. Bring day-to-day insights together to shape the future beyond the daily grind.

Hammer and Champy's business process redesign

The aim of a lot of strategy is to improve the performance of the business. Processes connect different parts of the business so if you improve those processes you will improve the overall business. It is argued that radical improvement requires radical re-engineering.

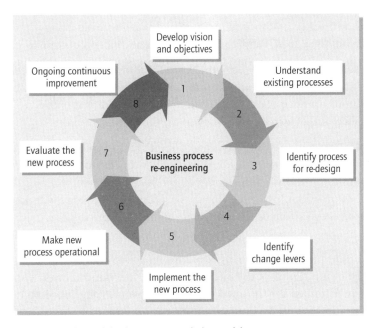

Hammer and Champy's business process redesign model

Source: Adapted from Vakola, M., Rezqui, Y. and Wood-Harper, T., 'The condor business process re-engineering model', *Managerial Auditing Journal*, 15, 42–46, Stockholm University, 2000

How to use

The idea here is that many attempts to improve the performance of organisations waste effort because they don't improve the processes through which people work. The more extreme version of BPR is that many processes should be removed (along with the people who do the work) because they don't add anything valuable.

Basic BPR involves getting a team together to review existing processes in light of strategic vision and objectives. These are redesigned and then implemented, at which point people follow new processes which are then evaluated and continuously improved.

Re-engineering received a lot of criticism and disappointing results from which valuable lessons emerged. Processes have to be understood well enough *in context* so the consequences of changing them can be anticipated. Teams need a mixture of rule-breakers and those who value those rules to avoid doing more harm than good. People are more important than processes.

Remember that process methodologies offer solutions when used intelligently, but many solutions taken to an extreme become problems once again. More than one organisation has choked on a fat meal of lean techniques fried in process-heavy butter.

Motorola was a strong advocate of Six Sigma methods but this did not save their market leadership. The IBM CEO who championed Business Process Improvement methods also led them to a multibillion-dollar loss. Even rigorous process methodology will not protect you from dumb strategy or failure to adapt.

Yet it is equally true that smart strategists can use process methods to provide, and adapt, available means to accomplish desirable ends. Think of the hugely successful Cleveland Clinics, who are described as a 'hospital trying to be Toyota'. They deliberately seek to improve patient care while reducing costs by standardising processes.

Michaud and Thoenig's strategic orientation

Different organisations have different perceptions of how much room there is for shaping their own future – through strategy and actions. They also respond in different ways to the perceptions about strong or weak external constraints.

	Short term	Long term
Strong pressure	Mercenary	Organic
Weak pressure	Fragmented	Self-sufficient

Michaud and Thoenig's strategic orientation

Source: Adapted from Michaud, C. and Thoenig, J. C., *Making Strategy and Organization Compatible*, Palgrave Macmillan, 2003

How to use

The idea is that different organisations have different perceptions of how much choice they have for their strategic actions. Anyone could decide to do anything, but in practice some people feel constrained by various things that are external or internal to the organisation. From this come different strategy-creating styles (or orientations).

- *Mercenary* – Your organisation perceives external pressure (in the market or from investors) as strong. In response, it adopts a very short-term approach to exploiting (and coping) with the external pressures. Managers reach outside of the organisation for answers and for people who can help. The art is in combining external (and temporary) talents in ways that meet market needs.

■ *Organic* – Your organisation perceives external pressure as strong but in response takes a long-term approach. Leaders argue that internal skills and cultural capabilities can be developed that are better at dealing with external pressure. Innovation and flexibility are built in so that the organisation uses the talents of all its employees to create and cope with opportunities.

■ *Fragmented* – Your organisation has responded to what are perceived to be weak external pressures by becoming quite set in its ways. It has lost the ability to adapt to new market changes and instead expends its energies on short-term efforts to appease various functional rivalries. Infighting is often the result since very few people see any pressure to start working together.

■ *Self-sufficient* – Your organisation sees weak external pressures but responds by looking for its own internal pressures (or desires) to innovate and change. It may feel safe but it still wants to achieve something over the long term. It wants to grow and to accomplish something worthwhile or notable. People who can 'create' futures worth pursuing are valued more than people who wait for something to happen.

You can use this model to consider what kind of organisation you belong to, and what kind of strategy will be typical. You can then decide on whether the organisational perception of external pressure is accurate. And you can look at whether the response to external pressure is desirable.

There may be reasons to try to shift the focus to one that is shorter or longer term depending on the true level of external pressure, the future likely level of external pressure, and the individual and group desire to make a difference or cope with politics.

Burgelman and Grove's strategy bet model

Some strategic initiatives can be planned and induced as part of the main organisation. Other opportunities have to be pursued autonomously. The balance between induced and autonomous initiatives will depend on market dynamics and available cash reserves.

Burgelman and Grove's strategy bet model

Source: Adapted from Burgelman, R. A. and Grove, A. S., 'Let chaos reign, then reign in the chaos – repeatedly: managing strategic dynamics for corporate longevity', *Strategic Management Journal*, John Wiley & Sons, 2007. Reproduced with permission of Blackwell Publishing

How to use

It's difficult for the organisation to pursue multiple strategic initiatives at the same time. Yet if everything is managed centrally there are emergent opportunities that will be missed. The answer is to make some resources available to autonomous initiatives.

You can alter the balance of resources according to the level of dynamism (or change) in the market. If the level of change is very high then you will need more autonomous initiatives to be able to cope with unforeseen opportunities. If the level of change is very low or you are in a dominant position, you may need fewer autonomous initiatives.

You will also consider the level of validation undertaken on an autonomous opportunity and the proportion of your cash reserves the autonomous opportunity will require in investment. If you haven't done your homework and you don't have enough cash to cover the complete loss of your investment, then it's a desperate bet. If you have done your homework and you still don't have enough funds then you may choose to bet the company.

It is generally wise to only speak about betting the company *after* that gamble is successful, but specifically it is not all that clever to bet the company at all. Steve Ballmer, ex-CEO of Microsoft, claimed that Windows 8 was a 'bet the company' move but he still had sufficient cash reserves to make it more of a safe bet.

The ex-CEO of BlackBerry, Thorsten Heins, similarly claimed that their 2013 phones were 'bet the company' attempts – and this appeared to be true, for when the bet failed, the company ran out of money. If he didn't sufficiently validate the gamble, it was perhaps even a desperate bet. He seemed to bet the whole company on a hunch.

You need time to change. If you bet too much cash you reduce the time available to you to get your strategy working. If you waste too much time, you may reduce the cash – and other resources – available to make your strategy possible.

Steve Jobs, Apple CEO, claimed he waited for 'the next big thing' and was, as a result, able to grab the opportunity presented by the iPod and iPhone. This wait-to-bet approach allowed him to get ready to bet – both by validating opportunities and by preparing capabilities necessary to grab those opportunities when they eventually arrived.

Argyris's double and single loop learning

Strategy involves guessing about the future and then acting on those guesses. You don't know what's going to happen but you plan and try to accomplish those plans. Ideally you try to learn from your mistakes (and successes) at a deeper level that informs future actions.

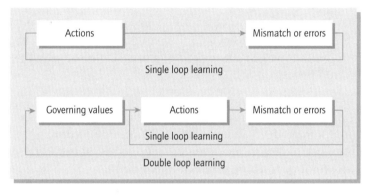

Argyris's double and single loop learning model

Source: Adapted from Argyris, C., 'The executive mind and double-loop learning', *Organizational Dynamics*, 11(2), 5-22, Elsevier Ltd, 1982

How to use

Strategic plans can lead to learning. Each time something works or doesn't work it can teach a lesson. The question is whether the learning stays at the operational level where actions are taken or whether the learning can provide lessons for the whole organisation. In particular, it's helpful if the governing values and strategic thinking of the company gets smarter.

Think about the last year. Consider how the strategy worked and did not work. Look for deeper lessons that can help strategy produce better results next time. Talk to people at the management and operational levels to see what really happened. Often lessons are learned on the front line that never make their way back up to the leadership teams.

Make sure your strategy process considers lessons during and at the end of each year. Were there any problems? Was the strategy altered to allow the company to achieve its financial results? Was the strategy ignored, leading to higher (or lower) performance? Are there contradictions between logic used to put the strategy together and logic leading to accomplishments? The aim is to connect strategy with action and the lessons that lead from both.

The CEO of Target, second largest discount retailer in the USA, announced the decision to expand into Canada during 2010. They purchased a failed discounter, Zellers, and opened refitted Target stores in 133 locations in 2013. Two years later, the old CEO was fired and the new CEO shut down the entire Canadian subsidiary with 17,000 jobs lost.

Some Canadian competitors took actions to alter some of their governing values to match Target's top-brands-at-low-prices approach to products and pricing. This double loop learning took place before Target even opened because competitors knew they were coming for several years before they arrived.

Meanwhile, Walmart Canada started a price war, sticking with actions close to their strengths that discomforted Target. And other rivals stocked products to match tastes and demands with know-how that Target Canada had not yet gained.

Target Canada launched too big, too quickly with the result that they learned too little, too slowly. They did not have the time to adjust their governing values to meet the demands of Canada. They did not take the time to play to their strengths – shelves were left empty of products that were advertised. They appeared in denial about the necessity of a fully functioning e-commerce website.

And despite employees – and customers – knowing all of this, leaders did not appear capable of learning fast enough. They did not learn sufficiently quickly from errors in implementation. They did not learn deep enough from mismatches between strategy and action.

Mintzberg's deliberate and emergent strategy

Not every intended strategy will be realised. Not all realised strategy comes from deliberate strategy. This is how strategy really happens. It is a mixture of what you plan and what is done that is not part of the plan. Understanding this helps you to be a better strategist.

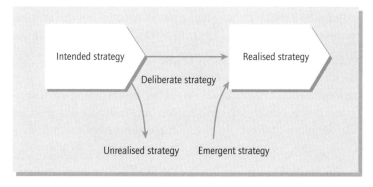

Mintzberg's deliberate and emergent model

Source: Adapted from Mintzberg, H., *Strategy Safari*, Pearson Education, 2009. With additional permission from Henry Mintzberg Ltd

How to use

It's helpful to understand the differences between planning something deliberately and what actually happens. This understanding frees you from excessive faith in planning and improves your strategic thinking.

First, consider what the company has been trying to accomplish over the past few years – or longer if you can find the information. Look at past annual reports. Talk to people who have been around for a while. Which parts of the strategy have turned out the way they were planned? Which parts have emerged from the actions of employees or reactions to competitors?

Extend the discussion to your team. Look for patterns over time. Try to find recognisable phases or stages of corporate history. When did you grow? When did you plateau? When did you enter new markets or countries?

Think about where the ideas came from that helped the company to grow. Where there any accidents along the way? Did luck play a part? Were there unanticipated opportunities that helped you grow?

Take Chipotle Mexican Grill as an example. The intended strategy of its founder, Steve Ells, was to raise funds for a fine dining restaurant by running a temporary takeaway. The deliberate strategy of selling 100 burritos per day on a university campus was way more successful than planned. They sold 1000 a day in the first month.

Putting the unrealised strategy of fine dining to one side, the CEO decided to grab the more exciting opportunities in the emergent strategy – what came to be known as fast casual dining. He had almost stumbled across a combination of fine dining sensibilities, the simplicity of street cooking and assembly line efficiency.

Now with 1700 locations, Chipotle still has only four items on the menu, no freezers, no microwaves or even can openers. Their ingredients arrive fresh and are prepared on site. The company has successfully developed emergent strategies, stuff that works, into intended strategies, what they try to do formally in each new store.

Johnson's white space model

There are ideas that you will create during the strategy process that do not lead to action. Sometimes this is because the idea is not a good fit for the organisation. Other times it's because the idea is not a good fit for your existing customers. Are these ideas wasted?

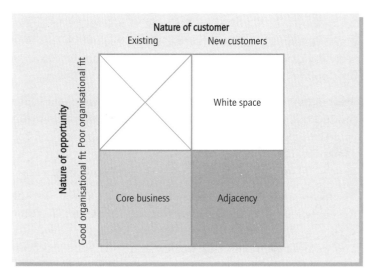

Johnson's white space model

Source: Adapted from Johnson, M. W., *Seizing the White Space: Business model innovation for growth and renewal*, Harvard Business School Publishing, 2010

How to use

After generating new ideas or opportunities, consider how they can be used. Are they part of your core business, with a good fit to what your organisation can already do and what your traditional customers buy? Or are they adjacent to your core business, with a good fit to what your organisation can already do but requiring new customers or significant changes to how you market to existing customers?

If they are not a good fit to your organisation, what are you going to do with the opportunities? You can just forget about them, of course, but you may be wasting really valuable ideas. You may also leave the door open to competitors who can come after your existing customers.

Think about how to protect yourself from others who come up with the same idea. You could develop new capabilities or protect the idea. If the idea cannot be used by you then consider how you can sell the intellectual property now or in the future.

Nintendo refused to enter the growing smartphone gaming market despite pressure to do so. First, because it might be a poor organisational fit – since it had no experience in this area. And second, because it might cannibalise existing handheld sales or disappoint existing customers. At best it was a risky white space.

Behind the scenes, DeNA, one of Japan's largest smartphone games producers, spent several years convincing Nintendo that they could partner with them. Together they would provide a good organisational fit to the new market – and games that were attractive to new and existing customers. Together they could grow.

The idea went from being a must-avoid to being a must-try. And the Nintendo CEO announced recently that Nintendo favourites such as Mario, Zelda and Donkey Kong will appear on smartphones and tablets. This creative new strategy is possible because they can now see how to make it work both as an adjacent and a core business.

Prahalad and Hart's bottom of the pyramid

It's easy to think that the only worthwhile markets are the people with the most money. Lots of businesses make that mistake. They move ever higher, looking for customers with the famous 'high net worth' and ignore much bigger total opportunities.

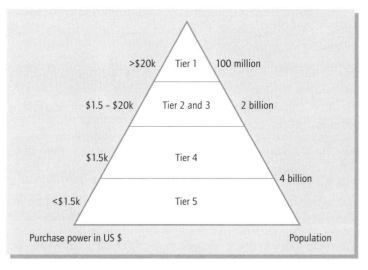

Prahalad and Hart's bottom of the pyramid model
Source: Adapted from Prahalad, C. K., *The Fortune at the Bottom of the Pyramid*, Pearson Education Ltd, 2010

How to use

The idea here is that the bottom of the global pyramid is a much more attractive market than it first appears. There are 4 billion or so who earn less than $2 a day and this market has a significant value. Instead of looking at the bottom of the pyramid as a problem or as recipients of charity, they offer valuable economic opportunities to corporations and entrepreneurs.

According to the model, those at the bottom of the pyramid (the relatively poor) are brand conscious, connected via mobile technology and very open to innovation. Those brands that establish themselves now will continue to grow with the growth at the bottom of the pyramid – which is much greater than the growth at the top of the pyramid.

Growth strategy should consider developing markets at the bottom of the pyramid. This development includes innovating so that the performance/price mix is radically improved, educating customers about product benefits and making the technology as simple, powerful and resilient as possible. It also offers opportunities to develop products that can be much better than existing products sold to the top of the pyramid.

There have been criticisms that bottom-of-the-pyramid success stories tend to take place higher up the pyramid – but this would still mean that markets are being developed in developing economies.

The ideal mix often localises production to keep prices attainable, while also adjusting to local tastes and usage patterns. Gillette famously redesigned its razors to lower costs and achieve a clean shave with a minimum of water – even in the street. Coca-Cola reduced the size of its Maaza Mango drink and its price to 8 cents.

China targeted bottom-of-the-pyramid infrastructure projects that become attractive when delivering benefits to thousands or millions of users. Similarly, Africa, the 'mobile-only' continent, moved directly to mobile phones without passing by fixed-line networks. Samsung and Huawei sell $20 smartphones to win in developing markets now enjoying more than double the growth in the rest of the world.

Stacey's strategy from complexity

You want the benefits of complexity for ideas and knowledge creation but you usually don't want to tip into full-blown chaos. And you want simplicity for getting the most out of the strategy you have discovered, but not so much that there is never anything new.

Stacey's strategy from complexity

Source: Stacey, R. C., *Strategic Management and Organisational Dynamics: the challenge of complexity to ways of thinking about organisations*, Pearson Education, 2010

How to use

The idea here is to understand that strategy is created (and used) in a context. The situation outside the company has different levels of uncertainty or certainty. The situation inside the company has different levels of agreement and disagreement over what to do next. The mix of certainty and agreement levels gives you a context for strategy and decision making.

If you are facing high levels of uncertainty and disagreement over what to do about it, then you may be at the edge of chaos. You may have the added problem that people are in denial about what is happening (or not happening). Somehow you need to reduce either uncertainty or disagreement down to levels where people can respond creatively to external uncertainty.

If there is too much agreement then you risk sleepwalking into problems because your group (team, company or nation) cannot see alternatives. If there is very high certainty in the market this may make strategy easy (but exceptional profits difficult) if you follow the crowd. Or you can use complacency in the market to create new markets and new rules.

Until recently, various competitors in the Swiss watch industry declared their strong agreement about the low threat posed to them by smart watches. The attraction to leaders is that decisions seem simple. The more uncertain the environment, the more tempting it can be to agree with each other that everything is under control.

In the past, hundreds of Swiss watchmakers disappeared because they thought quartz watches offered no threat. After the damage was done, they moved to a more complicated – and realistic – world view. They launched Swatch, which became the world No. 1. Others established luxury brands that captured 50% of global watch profits while producing only 2% of the world's watches.

The financial success of luxury brands attracted the attention of Apple – eager to find a new high margin product. Such an attack might have pushed Swiss watch firms back into denial or anarchy. To avoid this and to deal with the zone of complexity, Tag Heuer has partnered with Google and others who can lend hi-tech expertise.

Hart's sustainability value framework

If you care about your world, then you might also care about shaping a sustainable future. Equally, if the resources your strategy needs are no longer available then your strategy is unsustainable. Either of these reasons should be enough to make you consider the sustainability of your strategy.

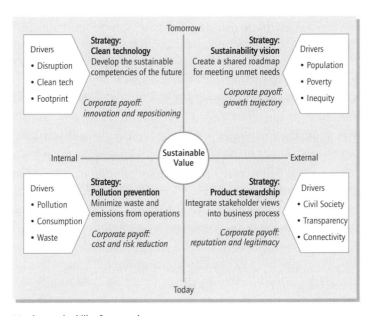

Hart's sustainability framework
Source: Adapted from Hart, S. L., 'Creating Sustainable Value', www.stuartlhart.com

How to use

Start by better understanding the sustainability of your existing strategy. You can look inside at the internal drivers – and the state-of your organisation. Then at the external drivers – and the situation – outside of your organisation. Consider what is happening today – and what is likely to happen tomorrow, if trends continue.

Instead of viewing sustainability as only a question of expensive ethics or costly regulations, consider the strategic benefits and possibilities now and in the future. What impact do you have on the external world? What impact does the external world have on you – and your desirable future? Strategy can't be separated from its interdependence with human society and the environment. So it makes sense to figure out how to make them work well together.

The shallowest approach is probably the product stewardship one – where your strategy is about image and is motivated by looking good in the here and now. Or you might use more efficient technologies as a way of reducing costs – and preventing pollution.

At a deeper level, you could take a strategic focus on developing approaches to clean technology that can create new advantages – putting you in a better position through innovation. Or, you could go much, much further and deliver a big-picture sustainability vision – changing some part of the wider system to really help the world.

You might start with an attempt to look good – like offering to plant trees for every flight purchased, as Delta airlines did. Be careful though, because there's a risk of disappointing – or angering – the external groups you wish to impress. It's often smarter to combine efforts to adopt efficient technologies, giving you both internal cost-savings and something more substantial to help your reputation.

As an ambitious, world-loving strategist, you can also work towards bigger opportunities for you and your planet. You can either develop cleaner technologies or approaches – as Toyota did with fuel cells – to give you an innovation-based advantage. Or, as with Tesla's work on a complete renewable energy network, try to completely reimagine, and re-engineer, some part of the human world so it is sustainable – or at least significantly less damaging.

House of strategy

Some people are motivated by a vision of the future they are trying to build. Some are more interested in the mission that they try to accomplish each and every day. Others are inspired by the values they are living by – or the goals they are pursuing – as they do their work. Not one of these is necessarily a strategy, but they can all help.

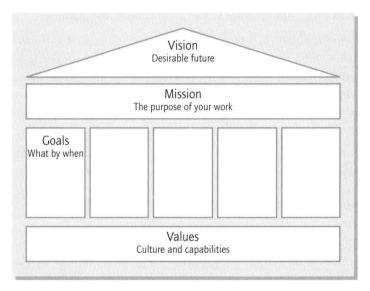

House of strategy

How to use

Find out if your company has already published an official filled-in version of the strategy house. They are often to be found on the corporate website – BMW has one, and so does Coca-Cola. If one doesn't exist, try to fill in a blank version with any existing statements about vision, mission, values and goals. Get it all in one place.

Start thinking about each component. Does the vision clearly describe a desirable future? How well does the mission help people to know what they are trying to achieve on a daily basis? How well do the highlighted goals flow from the mission and vision? Are the values so generic that they are valueless – or will they encourage a specific way of working that makes a valuable contribution? Note down your initial thoughts and highlight strengths, weaknesses, threats and opportunities. What works? What doesn't?

Stick your page up on a wall. Hand out copies to your colleagues. Use it for a team meeting. How does it relate to your day-to-day work? How can it guide your efforts to contribute new ideas? Which parts can be shared with customers and partners? If people outside the company know what you're trying to achieve, how can this lead to success?

Some people add so many extra layers that it becomes hard to read, hard to understand and impossible to remember. Like all tools, it is only useful if it helps you think and act strategically. Better to re-move anything that confuses rather than contributes – you don't *need* a formal vision, or a mission, goals and official values.

Tesla, manufacturer of electric cars and more, doesn't have a public vision or mission statement. Their 'goal is to accelerate the advent of sustainable transport by bringing compelling mass market electric cars to market as soon as possible'. This is a clear statement of purpose that has guided their strategic actions over the past decade.

When BMW realigned their strategy – known by the acronym Number ONE – they drew up a Strategy House that is still used. Their leadership team wanted to encourage each of their 100,000 people to contribute creatively to making the strategy work.

Their vision is to be the 'leading provider of premium products and premium services for individual mobility' in contrast to their historic role as a manufacturer. Their mission is to make the best use of new opportunities and new efficiencies to 'guarantee BMW's lead over competitors as well as the power and independence to shape the company's future actively'.

The BMW goals include growth, shaping the future, profitability and access to technologies and customers. Each of these, in turn, is supported by twelve values and what BMW hopes is a blend of company culture and capabilities well adapted to their mission, vision and goals.

Innovation + strategy = adaptability

The Strategy Book works well with *The Innovation Book* and *Adaptability*. So it's worth understanding how they fit together.

- *Innovation* is about creating new ideas and making those new ideas useful. It's a form of practical creativity that extends human ability beyond what was previously possible.

- *Strategy* is about shaping the future. It's about finding the smartest, shortest way to desirable ends with available means. It is our ability to act on imagined alternatives.

- *Adaptability* is about *recognising* the need to adapt, *understanding* the necessary adaptation and then adapting as *needed*. All success is successful adaptation. You can adapt to your situation or adapt your situation to your desires and dreams.

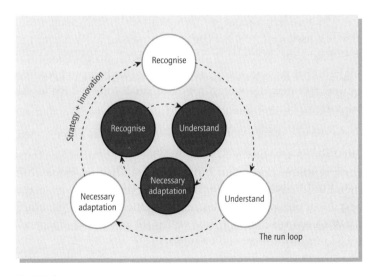

The RUN loop

The books share principles but only a few models and examples. You can bring the ideas in the three books together. Think like a strategist, create like an innovator and transcend limitations through a high-adaptability, high-achievement focus.

Final words

'The future cannot be predicted, but futures can be invented.'

Dennis Gabor, Nobel Prize in Physics

The principles in this book are based on the advice of the greatest strategic thinkers through the centuries and cutting-edge wisdom from the world's leading strategy researchers. Everything has been selected with great care. Each model in the strategist's toolkit is worth understanding and putting into practice. I guarantee this will be a valuable investment of your time, which will pay you rich dividends.

This isn't a book you should read, put down and forget about. It's a book about living strategy for the real world. So it is important that it is used well. Write in the margins, read it in the bath, stuff it in your overnight bag. It doesn't matter if it gets wrecked. It matters that you can use it and gain the knowledge to become a powerful strategic thinker who sees the small scale and the world-wide as one big powerful picture.

Then you will start to see the past, present and future as connected. You will be able to link the resources you have with the events that happen around you. And you will be able to shape those events by reacting intelligently and spontaneously to them.

'The people who get on in this world are those who get up and look for the circumstances they want, and if they can't find them, they make them.'

George Bernard Shaw

Further reading

Argyris, C. (1982). The Executive Mind and Double-Loop Learning. *Organization Dynamics*.

Barney, J. (2015). 15 firm resources and sustained competitive advantage. *International Business Strategy: Theory and Practice*, 283.

Bartlett, C. A. and Sumantra, G. (2012). *Managing Across Borders: The transnational solution* (Second Revised Edition). Cornerstone Digital.

Bingham, C. and Eisenhardt, K. (2014). Heuristics in strategy and organizations: response to Vuori and Vuori. *Strategic Management Journal*, 35(11), 1698–1702.

Burgelman, R. and Grove, A. (2007). Let Chaos Reign, Then Rein in Chaos – Repeatedly. *Strategic Management Journal*.

Burns, T. and Stalker, G. (1994). *The Management of Innovation*. Oxford University Press.

Calhoun, L. and Tedeschi, R. (eds) (2014). *Handbook of Posttraumatic Growth:* Research and Practice. Routledge.

Charan, R., Bossidy, L. and Burck, C. (2012). *Execution: The discipline of getting things done*. Random House.

Christensen, C. M. (2009). *The Innovator's Prescription: A disruptive solution for healthcare*. McGraw-Hill.

Christensen, C. M. (2013). *The Innovator's Dilemma: when new technologies cause great firms to fail*. Harvard Business Review Press.

Cialdini, R. (2007) *Influence: The Psychology of Persuasion*. Harper Business.

Clegg, S., Carter, C., Kornberger, M., and Schweitzer, J. (2011). *Strategy: Theory and Practice*, Sage Publications.

Cohen, M. D., March, J. G. and Olsen, J. P. (1972). A garbage can model of organizational choice. *Administrative Science Quarterly:* 1–25.

Cohen, W. (2004). *The Art of the Strategist*. AMACOM.

Collins, J. (2001). *Good to Great: Why some companies make the leap ... and others don't*. Random House.

Cummings, S. and Wilson, D. (2003). *Images of Strategy*. Blackwell Publishing.

Dagnin, G. B. (ed) (2012). *Handbook of Research on Competitive Strategy*. Edward Elgar Publishing.

Davidson, M. (1995). *The Grand Strategist*. MacMillan Publishing.

DeWit, B.and Meyer, R. (2014). *Strategy: An International Perspective*. Cengage Learning EMEA; 5th Revised edition.

DeRond, M. amd Thietart, R-A. (2007). Choice, chance and inevitability in strategy. *Strategic Management Journal*, 28(5), 535.

Floyd, S. W., Roos, J., Jacobs, C. D. and Kellermans, F. W. (eds) (2009). *Innovating Strategy Processes*. John Wiley & Sons.

Freedman, L. (2013). *Strategy: A History*. Oxford University Press.

Gavetti, G. (2012). Perspective: towards a behavioral theory of strategy. *Organizational Science*, 23, 1: 267–85.

Geroski, P. amd Markides, C. (2005). *Fast Second: How smart companies bypass radical innovation to enter and dominate new markets*. Jossey-Bass.

Golsortkhi, D., Rouleau, L., Seidl, D. and Vaara, E. (eds) (2010). *Cambridge Handbook of Strategy as Practice*. Cambridge University Press.

Grove, A. (1999). *Only the Paranoid Survive: How to exploit the crisis points that challenge every company*. Crown Business.

Hafsi, T. and Thomas, H. (2005). The Field of Strategy: In Search of a Walking Stick. *European Management Journal*, 23(5), 507–19.

Heracleous, L. (2003). *Strategy and Organization*. Cambridge University Press.

Hickson, D., Wilson, D. and Butler, R. (eds) (2001). *The Bradford Studies of Strategic Decision Making*. Ashgate.

Hickson, D., Wilson, D. and Miller, S. (2004). Beyond planning: Strategies for successfully implementing strategic decisions. *Long Range Planning*, 37, 3, 201–18.

Hodgkinson: G. and Healey, M. (2001). Psychological foundations of dynamic capabilities: reflexion and reflection in strategic management. *Strategic Management Journal*, 32(13), 1500–1516.

Hoffman, R. C. (1989). Strategies for corporate turnarounds: What do we know about them? *Journal of General Management*, 14, 3: 46–66.

Hrebiniak, L. (2005). *Making Strategy Work*. Wharton School Publishing.

Johnson, G., Whittington, R., Scholes, K., Angwin, D. and Regner, P. (2013). *Exploring Strategy* (Tenth Edition), FT Prentice Hall.

Johnson, M. (2010). *Seizing the White Space*. Harvard Business Press.

Kahneman, D. and Klein, G. (2009). Conditions for intuitive expertise: a failure to disagree. *American Psychologist*, 64(6), 515.

Kahneman, D. and Klein, G. (2010). Strategic decisions: when can you trust your gut? *McKinsey Quarterly*, 13, 1–10.

Kaplan, R. S. and Norton, D. P. (2005). *Creating the Office of Strategy Management*. Division of Research, Harvard Business School.

Kiechel, W. (2010). *The Lords of Strategy*. Harvard Business School Publishing.

Kim, W. Chan and Mauborgne, R. (2015). *Blue Ocean Strategy* (Expanded Edition). Harvard Business Press.

Lafley, A. G. and Martin, R. L. (2013). *Playing To Win*. Harvard Business Review Press.

Liteman, M., Campbell, S. and Liteman, J. (2006). *Retreats that Work: Everything you need to know about planning and leading great offsites*. John Wiley & Sons.

Lynch, R. (2005). *Corporate Strategy*. FT Prentice Hall.

Markides, C. and Geroski, P. (2005). *Fast Second*. Jossey-Bass.

McGee, J., Thomas, H. and Wilson, D. (2005). *Strategy: Analysis & Practice*. McGraw-Hill.

Menz, M. and Scheef, C. (2014). Chief strategy officers: Contingency analysis of their presence in top management teams. *Strategic Management Journal*, 35, 3: 461–71.

Mintzberg, H., Ahlstrand, B. and Lampel, J. (1998). *Strategy Safari*. FT Prentice Hall.

Mirabeau, L. and Maquire, S. (2014). From autonomous strategic behavior to emergent strategy. *Strategic Management Journal*, 35(8), 1202–29.

Nadkarni, S., Chen, T. and Chen, J. (2015). The clock is ticking! Executive temporal depth, industry velocity and competitive aggressiveness. *Strategic Management Journal*.

Ohmae, K. (1982). *The Mind of the Strategist*. McGraw Hill.

Osterwalder, A. and Pigneur, Y. (2010). *Business Model Generation: A handbook for visionaries, game changers and challengers*. John Wiley & Sons.

Pascale, R. (1990). *Managing on the Edge*. Penguin Books.

Peters, T. and Waterman, R. (1982). *In Search of Excellence*. Profile Books.

Piao, M. and Zajac, E. (2015). How exploitation impedes the impels exploration: Theory and evidence. *Strategic Management Journal*.

Powell, T. Lovallo, D. and Fox, C. (2011). Behavioral strategy. *Strategic Management Journal*, 32, 13, 1369–86.

Reeves, M., Hannaes, K. and Janmejaya, S. (2015) *Your Strategy Needs A Strategy*. Harvard Business Press.

Rumelt, R. (2012). *Good Strategy/Bad Strategy: The difference and why it matters*. Profile Books.

Sarasvathy, S. D. (2001). Causation and effectuation: Toward a theoretical shift from economic inevitability to entrepreneurial contingency. *Academy of Management Review*, 26, 2: 243–63.

Sarasvathy, S. D. (2006). What to do next? The cast for non-predictive strategy. *Strategic Management Journal*, 27, 10: 981

Schoenberg, R., Collier, N. and Bowman, C. (2013). Strategies for business turnaround and recovery: A review and synthesis. *European Business Review*, 25, 3: 243–62.

Sloan, J. (2013) *Learning to Think Strategically*. Routledge; 2nd edition.

Stacey, R. (2010). *Strategic Management and Organisational Dynamics: The Challenge of Complexity (To Ways of Thinking About Organisations)*. Financial Times/ Prentice Hall.

Sklansky, D. and Schoonmaker, A. (2010). *DUCY? Exploits, Advice, and Ideas of the Renowned Strategist*. Two Plus Two Publishing.

Stalk, G. and Lachenaeur, R. (2004). *Hardball*. Harvard Business School Press.

Suarez, F. F., Grodal, S. and Gotsopoulos, A. (2015) Perfect timing? Dominant category, dominant design and the window of opportunity for firm entry. *Strategic Management Journal*, 36, 3: 437–48.

Thietart, R-A. (2015). Strategy dynamics: Agency, path dependency and self-organized emergence. *Strategic Management Journal*, 36(9).

Thomas, H., Pettigrew, A. and Whittington, R. (2001). *Handbook of Strategy and Management*. Sage Publications.

Thomas, H., McGee, J. and Wilson, D. (2010). Strategy: *Analysis and Practice* (Second Edition). McGraw-Hill Higher Education.

Von Ghyczy, T., Von Oetinger, B. and Bassford, C. (2001). *Clausewitz on Strategy*. The Boston Consulting Group.

Whittington, R. (1993). *What is Strategy – And Does It Matter?* Routledge.

Zott, C. and Amit, R. (2015). Business model innovation: Toward a process perspective. *The Oxford Handbook of Creativity, Innovation and Entrepreneurship*, 395.

Acknowledgements

Thanks to the many thousands of people who have worked with me in strategy sessions around the world. Comparing strategy theory with strategy in the real world is the heart of *The Strategy Book*.

Particular thanks go to those who have offered comments and feedback throughout the writing process. And to those who have discussed strategy ideas with me over the years. They include Simon Collinson, Sotirios Paroutis, David Wilson, Jan-Henrik Andersson, Cesar Malacon and Mike Chitty.

Publisher's acknowledgements

We are grateful to the following for permission to reproduce copyright material:

Figure on page 169 adapted from Porter, M. E., 'How competitive forces shape strategy', *Harvard Business Review*, March/April 1979, courtesy of Harvard Business School Publishing; figures on pages 171 and 175 adapted with permission of the Free Press, a Division of Simon & Schuster, Inc. from *Competitive Advantage: Creating and Sustaining Superior Performance* by Porter, M. E. Copyright © 1985. All rights reserved; figure on page 179 adapted from Nonaka, I. and Takeuchi, H. *The Knowledge-Creating Company*, Oxford University Press, 1995; figure on page 185 adapted from Ansoff, I., 'Strategies of diversification', *Harvard Business Review*, 25(5), Harvard Business School Publishing, 1957; figure on page 187 adapted from the BCG Portfolio Matrix from the Product Portfolio Matrix, ©1970, The Boston Consulting Group (BCG); figure on page 189 adapted from Kim, W. C. and Mauborgne, R., *Blue Ocean Strategy: How to create an uncontested market space and make the competition irrelevant*, Harvard Business School Press, 2005; figure on page 191 adapted from Greiner, L. A., *Evolution and Revolution as Organizations Grow*, Harvard Business School Publishing, 1998; figure on page 193 adapted from De Wit, B., Meyer, R. and Heufens, P., *Strategy: Process, Content, Context: An International Perspective*, Cengage Learning, Inc., 2010; figure on p. 195 adapted from Cummings, S. and Wilson, D., *Images of Strategy*, Wiley-Blackwell, 2003; figure on p. 199 reproduced with the permission of The Free Press, a division of Simon & Schuster, Inc., from *A Force for Change: How Leadership Differs From Management* by Kotter, J. P. Copyright © 1990. All rights reserved, with additional permission from Kotter Associates, Inc.; figure on page 201 adapted from Kaplan,

R. S. and Norton, D. P., 'The balanced scorecard: measures that divide performance', *Harvard Business Review*, Harvard Business School Publishing, 2005; figure on page 203 adapted from Hrebiniak, L. G., *Making Strategy Work*, Wharton School Publishing, 2005; figure on p. 205 adapted from Vakola, M., Rezqui, Y. and Wood-Harper, T., 'The condor business process re-engineering model', *Managerial Auditing Journal*, 15, 42–46, Stockholm University, 2000; figure on page 207 adapted from Michaud, C. and Thoenig, J. C., *Making Strategy and Organization Compatible*, Palgrave Macmillan, 2003; figure on page 209 from Burgleman, R. A. and Grove, A. S., 'Let chaos reign, then reign in chaos - repeatedly: Managing strategic dynamics for corporate longevity', *Strategic Management Journal*, John Wiley & Sons, 2007. Reproduced with permission of Blackwell Publishing; figure on p. 211 adapted from Argris, C., 'The executive mind and double-loop learning', *Organizational Dynamics*, 11(2), 5–22, Elsevier Ltd, 1982; figure on p. 213 adapted from Mintzberg, H., *Strategy Safari*, Pearson Education Ltd, 2009, with additional permission from Henry Mintzberg Ltd; figure on page 215 adapted from Johnson, M. W., *Seizing the White Space: Business model innovation for growth and renewal*, Harvard Business School Publishing, 2010; figure on p. 217 adapted from Prahalad, C. K., *The Fortune at the Bottom of the Pyramid*, Pearson Education Ltd, 2010; figure on page 221 adapted from Hart, S. L., 'Creating Sustainable Value', www.stuarthart.com; courtesy of Stuart Hart.

In some instances we have been unable to trace the owners of copyright material, and we would appreciate any information that would enable us to do so.

Index